ON BEING A BIRD

The author, and then new World Champion, at Cuatro Vientos in
July 1952.

ON BEING A BIRD

PHILIP WILLS

David & Charles

Newton Abbot London North Pomfret (Vt) Vancouver

To Kitty

By the same author:
The Beauty of Gliding
Free as a Bird
The Inevitability of Confrontation
Where No Birds Fly

ISBN 0 7153 7426 5
Library of Congress Catalog Card Number 77-80133

First published 1953 by Max Parrish & Co Ltd

Printed in Great Britain by
Redwood Burn Limited
Trowbridge and Esher
for David & Charles (Publishers) Limited
Brunel House Newton Abbot Devon

Published in the United States of America
by David & Charles Inc
North Pomfret Vermont 05053 USA

Published in Canada
by Douglas David & Charles Limited
1875 Welch Street North Vancouver BC

CONTENTS

The author's acknowledgements are due to the Editors of *The Times*, *Aeronautics* and *Lilliput* for permission to reprint articles which have appeared in their pages, to Messrs John Murray for permission to use part of his contribution to Ann Douglas's *Gliding and Advanced Soaring*, and to Mr R. H. Swinn for permission to reprint part of his article on 'Dust Devils'. He is also grateful to the following for their courtesy in allowing him to reproduce photographs in their possession: Professor Fritschi, T. Heimgartner, The Royal Meteorological Society, Whites Aviation Ltd., New Zealand.

The author's greatest thanks are due to Anstace Goodhart, who drew the illustrations, and her brother Tony. Both of them were rocks throughout.

Mr Hugh Kendall and Dr R. S. Scorer have given much useful advice on some of the more technical aspects: the mistakes which remain are the author's own.

FOREWORD

BUCKINGHAM PALACE.

Is it any use?   That is the title of the first
chapter of this fascinating and instructive book.
The delightful story of the lady who lived near Cheddar
Gorge might have been told of any worthwhile leisure
activity.   I confess that I winced when I saw that
title.   I have sailed for fun in boats which are
quite useless for anything else.   I have played polo,
and that can hardly be described as a useful activity,
and I have now taken to driving a four in hand which
might only be remotely useful on the off chance that
the energy crisis reaches quite alarming proportions.

I can think of many other equally useless but
nonetheless enjoyable activities, but I believe it is
not the usefulness which counts, it is the challenge
to overcome the problems, the exhilaration of doing
it well and the tantalising inability to reach
perfection.   In this respect, gliding must be one
of the most satisfactory of leisure activities and
this book explains in lucid detail just what there is
to it.

Doers are not always writers, but this book proves
that the author controls his pen with the same flair
and enthusiasm as he flew his beloved gliders.

1976.

They say that everyone has it in them to write one good book. But when one actually starts to take 'them' at their word, doubts begin to creep in. Who are they anyway? Are they going to read it?

In so far as gliding is concerned, the world falls into three classes: a few thousand who do it, perhaps twenty times that number who would do it if only . . . and the remaining two thousand-odd million folk who don't even know what gliding is, and would not care if they did.

Let me say at once, therefore, what this book is not. It is not a technical text-book for the practising enthusiast. Indeed, our subject has nowadays become altogether too big a one for the whole scope to be contained in any one volume. As in so many other fields, ours has now become so large that separate books need to be written under each heading: meteorology, aerodynamics, training methods and operating techniques, constructional and repair methods, instrumentation, and so on.

This is not any one of those books: indeed, whatever some might think, I do not claim to be an expert on any one of these subjects, and on some of them I am positively dim.

What I am trying to do, therefore, is to paint a picture of the air as it seems to the man or woman who approaches it in silent flight, as a medium almost more than material, having a life and character of its own.

This has been attempted in the case of the sea, and by far more brilliant pens than mine, because man has been able for centuries to absorb the moods and character of the oceans from sailing craft and canoes in slow and contemplative fashion, and only later has it become comparatively remote from the decks of Atlantic greyhounds.

Man, however, has been brought to the air in the reverse order. The early flights of balloons and primitive gliders soon gave way to the noise and vibration of the powered craft, and man's senses thus bedevilled are incapable of absorbing the elusive flavours of this new medium. Only since the advent of soaring flight has it become possible to attempt the task I am now essaying.

The air is a truly vast canvas, and one extraordinarily difficult to convey intelligibly to others. I have therefore had to attempt the method of the Impressionists – to throw on blobs of colour in a way which, at first sight, may appear random, but which, if it comes off, will gradually build up a total picture of greater descriptive subtlety than can be achieved by more direct methods.

To understand our picture, the reader will have to learn some of our language, and this I hope he will do, without tears, as he reads on through the book. The plan, therefore, is to build up a picture by telling of various experiences, interspersing between each sufficient technical matter, told as simply as possible, to make each succeeding story comprehensible.

It is a formidable task and my only qualification to attempt it is that I have been well and truly bitten by the bug for longer than most. It is now over twenty years since my first launch, and in that time I have tried to learn enough of the subject to achieve my desire: to have as much fun as it is possible to extract from the most absorbing sport of all time.

There is a true story of a sailplane pilot who landed in the park of a large house somewhere near the Cheddar Gorge.

The lady of the house came out and, after the machine had been attended to, asked the pilot in, and proceeded to cross-examine him. After hearing all he had to say, she said: 'Well, I simply can't imagine what makes you waste your time in such an extraordinary way!' A little later, the tea was brought in, and as she poured it out, she remarked 'I am so sorry that my husband isn't here to meet you. He is out caving. . .'

Why glide? This is perhaps the first question shot at enthusiasts by the stranger. The question is one that is difficult to answer on the spot without being either boring or pompous. The man of my dreams, who always produces the right answer at the time, instead of an hour after the questioner has gone, would I think reply something on the following lines.

'You ask me, madam, what use is Gliding. Well, there are many useful things in the world, such as Uranium 235 or the Ministry of Supply or the latest detergent powder; and many useless ones, like the path of the moon dancing to the sea's horizon, or the smell of a wood on a summer's morning, or the Unfinished Symphony.

'You enquire in which camp Gliding stands and I think the true answer is that it has a foot in both. But as for me, I fly because I am fascinated by the ocean of the air, by its habits and moods, and in learning slowly to understand its curious ways. I suppose you could say that I love the air for itself, as a good husbandman loves the earth or the good sailor the sea. And in people of my way of thinking I find a companionship I need.'

'But', chips in my dream-lady (and just at the right moment), 'if you have this peremptory urge to fly, which occurs in no other land-animal I know of, and so must in itself indicate some psychological abnormality, why not fly an aeroplane, which I can see does in fact get you somewhere both literally and metaphorically?'

'It is possible', I reply, 'that I cannot explain to you what I am trying to communicate. Your tea has been excellent, and as my hostess I feel indeed grateful to you, but in our short conversation you have dropped more bricks than I may be able to pick up before you throw me out.

'Can you understand that you cannot learn the subtle flavours of the air by screaming, deafened and bejellied, behind five thousand odoriferous horses across the complaining sky? The powered aircraft provides the quickest, least tiring and most satisfactory way to deliver a business man to his board, or an atom bomb to Hiroshima. Its functions may quickest be summed up in the two words: death and dividends.

'So the satisfactions to be achieved from powered flight are quite different. They may include excellent things such as a desire to serve the community, or to exercise one's administrative or technical talents; they may develop admirable characteristics in a man, such as courage, devotion to duty, or the intellectual integrity of scientific or technical research. They may shade off into less worthy motives, such as to demonstrate power over more ordinary people, or even to show off to the girl-friend.

'But I don't leap into my sailplane when I want to go anywhere, or when I want to kill someone or to stop him killing me. I leap into my sailplane when I want to fly.

'So if you ask me why I glide, I glide because I must.'

At this point my dream-lady (who is also, I forgot to mention before, very beautiful) throws herself at my feet and begs to join my retrieving team.

But perhaps, after all, my dream-man is a pompous fellow, and certainly his diatribe will not produce any material support from the Powers that Be. And as the Powers that Be do support gliding (although not, in this country, what we call sporting gliding), there clearly are answers more satisfactory to the materialist than the one sketched above. Let us pass on to them.

Perhaps few people realise that man eventually discovered how to fly through the medium of gliders. For centuries he had dreamed of flight, and, since all the necessary materials were available, there was in fact nothing to prevent him achieving his dream a thousand years ago except for his miserably poor powers of observation. Instead of watching the classic simplicity of the gull soaring with motionless wings over the cliffs when the sea breeze blows towards the land, he got tangled up in the complexities of flapping flight and feathers.

It is, at first blush, a curious fact that, although a soaring bird, whilst actually soaring, is an incredibly efficient glider (so efficient that the modern aerodynamicist still cannot explain how he achieves his performance), as a powered aircraft the efficiency of the *flapping* bird is very low indeed.

One can only appreciate this to the full by putting a model in a smoke wind-tunnel, when the mess of complex vortices produced in the air behind the flapping wing has to be seen to be believed.

But with a little more thought, it can be seen that Nature has never managed to achieve the efficiency of a man-made machine designed to achieve a single purpose; in the field of transport, possibly this is because of her extraordinary failure to use the device of the wheel. A man on a pedal cycle can move himself from A to B with notably less expenditure of energy than a man running at the same speed. Similarly, an aircraft with fixed wings propelled by a rotating airscrew (or turbine) requires only a fraction of the power which would be needed by an equivalent aircraft with flapping wings.

Nature might retort that her product must also be able to fold its wings, refuel itself, be superbly manœuvrable both in the air and on the ground, reproduce itself and so forth. But that is another story.

Even when Lilienthal and the other pioneers started experimenting with fixed wings, it seems that they still failed to look up at the myriad birds soaring overhead, and the gawky outlines of those early aircraft developed only slowly into the bird-like shapes of today. Man had to work out the bird all over again, by mathematics and experiment, and after thirty years' calculation he looked up from his slide-rule with the answer, which he then saw had been visible in the sky over his head the whole time.

At about the time that Lilienthal and Pilcher were experimenting with gliders, Otto was also working on his cycle, and the internal combustion engine was born. Consequently no sooner had the Wright brothers achieved a satisfactorily controllable glider than they eagerly put a little engine in it, with the results we see around us and overhead today.

So the glider was pushed into the background until the Germans brought it out again in the 1920's when, having been prohibited by the Treaty of Versailles from operating powered craft, they reverted to gliders. I don't believe that they had the faintest idea of what this was to lead to, of the consequent advances in meteorological knowledge, in aerodynamics and structures. But the bald fact is that, little more than ten years later, they had trained the designers and the pilots on which they founded the Luftwaffe. In addition they had done something else which has not created the interest which it deserves: they had produced the first really airminded nation the world had seen.

In Britain in 1953 we have not nearly equalled the airmindedness of the German people in the late 1930's. You could not land near the smallest German village in those days without finding informed and enthusiastic assistance in the resulting crowd. And today, fifteen years later, there are tens of thousands of Germans hungering to fly again, at a time when, in Britain, the total membership of all light aeroplane and gliding clubs combined is a few thousand.

By joining the Air Training Corps, any boy between the ages of 16 and 18 can now obtain elementary gliding training at the public expense. This scheme has been running long enough to reach a high state of efficiency, and the most sceptical now acknowledge its irreplaceable value. But the majority of Service opinion still regards gliding as a lure through which to obtain recruits, without any direct training value for subsequent powered flying. This is probably true to the rather elementary stage to which glider training is at present restricted. But I am not sure that it is true in the

15

case of an advanced sailplane pilot, and I can produce some, necessarily limited, facts tending to indicate the reverse.

The 'Silver C' badge is generally acknowledged as the minimum standard to be achieved before a glider pilot is fully fledged. It is an International badge, and to achieve it the aspirant has to pass three tests: a distance flight of 50 kilometres, a climb of 1,000 metres (about 3,300 feet), and a duration flight of five hours.*

During the War, I was Director of Operations in Air Transport Auxiliary, an organisation of ferry pilots. The training courses needed to produce a ferry pilot qualified to fly every type of aircraft ranging from an elementary trainer to the largest bombers were, of course, tremendously costly. The time came when we accepted any volunteer for pilot duties who already held a Silver C, and after it was all over I analysed, as well as was possible, the training and ferrying records of the fourteen Silver C pilots who had joined. Over the four pre-war years, the gliding clubs had received a

---

* My average reader – that handsome, intelligent-looking fellow sitting over there with his attractive wife reading eagerly over his shoulder – has done a good deal of motoring on the Continent, but his flying has all been done in British aircraft. Thus he is equally at home in miles or kilometres where distances and speeds are concerned, but can visualise heights much better when expressed in feet.

Accordingly I have in each chapter used the system of measurement, for distances and speeds, appropriate to the countries concerned, but have kept to feet throughout for altitudes.

As a workaday conversion factor, I always multiply by 0·6. For kilometres to miles, 100 kilometres is very roughly 60 miles. For miles to kilometres, you add this to the number first thought of: 100 miles is nearly 100 + 60 = 160 kilometres.

My highbrow reader won't like any of this, but there will only be comparatively few of him, and anyway he is not half so good-looking.

An Avro 504 takes off with Kit Nicholson's Rhönsperber on aero-tow in the late 1930s.

A Minimoa.

Government subsidy amounting to £5,000 a year. The nation saved this amount on each of these fourteen pilots alone.

This of course is only a fraction of the assistance to the war effort of the civil gliding clubs, but one I happened to be close to. Club members fought and flew in every theatre of war. The more elderly formed the nucleus of instructors on which the A.T.C. was based in 1943. Nearly all club gliders and winches were requisitioned and formed their initial equipment. For at least six months a handful of high-performance sailplanes, requisitioned from pre-war clubs and private owners, formed the only flying equipment of the Airborne Army which later darkened the skies of Arnhem. One can say of the British gliding movement what the whaling companies say of the whale: 'They used every bit of it except the smell.' And the smell, which I think of as a combination of woodshavings and dope, we dreamed of until we could get back to it.

But although the British gliding movement gave its all it was a very small all, because it was a very small movement, and it went unnoticed in the tide of tremendous events. Thus, since the war, the subsidy has not been renewed, and the most that can be said (and it is a good deal) is that we have been left alone, and not regulated out of existence. Bureaucracy has forborne to touch us and turn us into stone.

If, instead of limited facilities for a limited age-bracket of young men, we had facilities available for everyone of either sex to progress as far as their talents led them, what would it cost, and what might we achieve? The answer must be vague, but for less than the annual cost of one medium bomber, we might produce a national consciousness of the air as vivid and valuable as the sea-consciousness of the times of the first Elizabeth.

An air-minded community does not, of course, merely consist of one with a high percentage of the population able to pilot an aircraft. It must provide a context sympathetic to the development of the designer, the technician, meteorologist, aircraft builder and repairer, and the plain all-rounder. A thriving gliding movement does all this.

There are some who say that there is no parallel between the sonic and supersonic pilot and aircraft and us potterers of the air. But we use the same air, and the more my airline pilot knows about the medium he operates in the more confidence I shall continue to have in him. There are many things about the air which can only be experienced in sailplanes. Including the love of it.

When war broke out, I joined Air Transport Auxiliary, which became the aircraft ferrying organisation for both flying services. Our first nine months, in which we were building up a complete flying service in miniature, were the most hectic of my life. By the summer of 1940 we were just beginning to see a faint possibility of some sort of order in the distance. I was O.C. No. 1 Ferry Pool at White Waltham.

One June day, with the preliminaries of the Battle of Britain just under way, I was summoned by our C.O., Commander D'Erlanger, and found him with an Air Commodore from Farnborough. To my considerable surprise, I was told that there was a highly secret and important job to be done urgently, involving the use of gliders, and asked if I was prepared to get my Minimoa out of store and come and take part. We were still appallingly overworked and understaffed in A.T.A. at the time, but it didn't take long to decide to accept this intriguing offer, which led me to the most fascinating experience of my war.

My old school friend, Mungo Buxton, then Wing Commander Buxton, who had first interested me in gliding in 1932, was in charge of our special-duty flight, which in due course assembled at Christchurch aerodrome, in Hampshire. When I arrived there, I blinked several times. We were just entering the greatest air-battle of all time, and almost the lowest ebb of our country's fortunes in this or any other war. Dunkirk was over, France had fallen, and the enemy were operating against us from airfields just across the Channel, where it was known he was preparing actual invasion of our island, which, by all common-sense standards, promised to be a walk-over. In the midst of all this, I found myself at what looked extremely like the opening day of a peace-time gliding meeting with the exception that the participants were in various kinds of uniform. Besides myself, oddly got up in the uniform of a civil airline pilot, there were Robin Fender, Peter Davis, Dougie Davie, and Carl Withall (who was soon recalled to operational duties), dressed as Pilot Officers. There were Slazenger and Pat Pringle, humbly disguised as A.C.2's, and Ruffle, a Corporal in Barrage Balloons. With affectionate pride we regarded an array of the best sailplanes we had: my Minimoa, two Viking I's, and the Viking II two-seater. Most startling of all, presiding with an air of octogenarian benignity over these were the prehistoric shapes of two Avro 504 biplanes, stalwarts of the First World War, looking as if someone had been robbing the historical section of the Science Museum in South Kensington. Our special duty was clearly something quite uniquely special.

In due course Buxton arrived and we were told the form. Special it was. For the first time, I heard of the existence of radar (then called Radio Direction-Finding, or R.D.F.).

I was astonished all through the war at the capacity of the Englishman to hold his tongue. In A.T.A. we were at the hub of most things. Every day our pilots went out and flew the length and breadth of the islands, yet never did any secret leak out through A.T.A. And here was a secret, involving strange masts and aerials sticking out of the landscape in highly obvious places, which I had never heard of, and one which clearly held the first ray of a rational hope that we might not, after all, follow France and the rest of Europe into defeat.

Already, nowadays, schoolchildren take radar and television for granted, and it may be hard to realise how incredible it was to hear that very high frequency radio waves had been discovered with the property of reflecting back from any object they might meet, and so positioning it on a luminous screen. As happened almost too often to ascribe merely to luck, this invention had been made just in time to make it possible that it might, by a supreme effort of technical skill and enthusiasm, be developed in time to save us. Our largest research station was located on, of all places, the cliffs overlooking Swanage, where it was now within sixty miles of an enemy possessing complete local air superiority. But there was certainly no time to move it, so we must work night and day and hope he would ignore it. Those whom the Gods wish to destroy they first make mad: in this, as in major later events, the enemy seemed insanely incompetent.

Our particular part in this extraordinary race of intellect against overwhelming force was as follows. The key Belgian fort of Eben Emael had fallen almost without a struggle during the rape of Belgium through its capture by a small number of glider-borne troops, taking advantage of the silence of their aircraft. It was known that similar preparations were in train as part of the forthcoming invasion of England. Enough was not yet known as to whether our R.D.F., at its then stage of development, was capable of picking up approaching gliders, made as they were largely of wood. If R.D.F. failed, a second important need was to find out whether our ordinary visual spotter system was likely to be able to give useful warning of the flight of such silent aircraft.

Our special duty therefore was to carry out dummy runs in our sailplanes, in front of the experimental scanners of Worth Matravers, and what made the duty so extra-special was the fact that, since these reflectors faced the sea, our flights would have to consist of being towed at 45 m.p.h. behind our antediluvian 504's to the maximum height of which they were capable – about 10,000 feet – as near to France as was possible, whilst still giving us height to get home. As the air was fairly thick at the time with enemy aircraft, with yellow warnings every half-hour or so and reds several times a day, it seemed fair comment when someone remarked dryly that he hoped the Germans knew the Rules of the Air and would give way to the right when they saw an oncoming glider on tow.

Worth Matravers was a jumble of huts, laboratories, gigantic reflectors and odd-shaped radio masts, located incongruously on one of the beauty-spots of England: high green fields rolling to the top of abrupt yellow-white cliff edges over which, peering down, one saw the sea beating the rocks at their foot 600 feet below. Besides the fortuitous advantage that the next-door field was large enough for the remarkably short take-off of the 504 with glider on tow, it was a fact – certainly not planned by its creators – that it was situated on an ideal hill-soaring site, for with the daily sea breeze blowing, strong upcurrents were obvious all along the crenellated line of cliffs. Although this did not at the time seem important from our point of view, it did a little later save me from what would otherwise have been, at the best, a tricky swim.

But the thing about Worth Matravers which put the most heart into me, and which compared with nothing I have felt before or since, was the atmosphere. I have always admired and liked the integrity and the enthusiasm of the research worker. But here, exposed to instant enemy attack at any hour of the day or night on a target which looked, and was, both easy and of the first importance, several hundreds of young men, looking like University students in open shirts and dirty grey flannel trousers, presided over by earnest professors and academicians, worked endless hours with a concentration of energy and enthusiasm I have never seen equalled. Such work can never seem – or be – orderly, yet out of this apparently confused bustle were coming results which from then on changed the history of the world.

With the siren going every few minutes, and the occasional sound of bombs on Weymouth or Swanage, the conscientious and accurate investigation of the properties of the magnetron might have seemed a burying of one's head in the sand, but these folk knew that nothing else being done at the time held greater hope of survival.

The next few weeks went like a dream.

To begin with we were practically grounded by an official prohibition to take off during an air-raid warning, and these were so frequent that for a day or so we hardly left the ground. The regulation was obviously no protection to us because if a warning occurred a minute after take-off, we could not be recalled, because we had no radio. So when Buxton was one day recalled to London for a conference, I as second-in-command was able to take advantage of my civilian status and consequent immunity from service discipline, to forget this regulation, which broke the impasse.

To avoid attracting the attention of the enemy more than necessary, we kept the aircraft at Christchurch, but every morning would tow the trailers up to Worth and rig the gliders, and the 504's would drop, as congruous as pterodactyls, out of the sky. Discussion and briefing of the day's work had usually been completed the night before, and we would quickly take off into the cloudless hazy blue which everyone remembers. The cliffs of Swanage would gradually fade into the haze behind, and as we gained height the circle of green-blue sea visible below would get smaller, until one seemed to be looking down through a small hole in the centre of a smoke-ring which extended to the horizon on all sides. Above the haze-ceiling visibility seemed unlimited, but there was nothing to see but the tow-line tying one to the apparently stationary shape of the gallant old crock ahead, etched against the cloudless blue and brilliant sky. The air was as smooth as sleep.

Our instruments, by modern standards, left something to be desired, bearing in mind the penalty of releasing too far away from our invisible home. Glider and aeroplane each possessed an ordinary magnetic compass, to get us to release point, and back again on course. To calculate our distance out we had our air-speed indicator, a wrist watch, and a hazy idea of wind speed and direction. For height, an altimeter. The performance of Minimoa was fairly well known, and should carry one in still air about 25 miles for every 5,000 feet of height. The performances of the Vikings, however, had never been measured, and we had to make an intelligent guess.

We would release about 40 miles out to sea: about 20 miles from the enemy coast. There are no upcurrents to be expected over the sea, so our return was a straight gliding descent. It was not feasible for the aeroplane to keep one friendly company on the way back, because our unseen watchers needed it to get out of the way as quickly as possible. So after release the 504 bore off to starboard and would return home by a wide circuit, out of sight. It was quite a moment when the aeroplane pilot waved one off, turned, and disappeared. Common sense told one that the glider on its own was slightly less conspicuous, and so slightly less vulnerable, than the two machines hung together; nevertheless one felt somewhat naked as the machine ruddered round on to course for the shrouded cliffs somewhere in the north. Time would pass, and pass again, with nothing but the needles of the air-speed indicator and altimeter to show one was moving through the dead-smooth smoky air, until a faint glint of white ahead would come and go, and come again and stay. Then the outlines of the cliffs would develop, the moment came when it was clear the machine would make it, the edge of the cliffs would slide below, and a few minutes later one grounded and ran eagerly to hear the results of the test.

Throughout these flights we never saw an enemy aircraft whilst we were airborne. This was not because they weren't there. One day, in the darkness of the tracking room, I watched Buxton on the screen take off, and commence his seaward climb. As he started to gain height, we saw the track of an enemy machine leaving the French coast and flying directly towards our crawling train. Remorselessly the two points of light approached each other, and for one agonising moment they fused. Then they separated again, and each proceeded unflurried on his divergent course. Buxton saw nothing, and it occurred to us that if the German pilot in 1940 looked over the side of his aircraft and saw in the no-man's-land of mid-channel a last-war Avro 504 towing a sporting German sailplane at 10,000 feet at 45 m.p.h., he probably put his hands before his eyes and drove madly away.

Worth were satisfied with what they saw, but they increasingly pressed us to cut our approaches lower and lower. They knew now that they could spot gliders at good heights, but still wanted to know if they could detect a really low arrival. So we pared and pared, until one day when the cliffs hazily loomed ahead I saw quite plainly that I could not possibly clear them. Worth was going to get its money's worth: what I was going to get seemed less certain, since there was no possibility of landing at the rocky foot of the cliffs.

Whilst still at least a mile out, I had sunk to the level of the cliff-top, then the encampment disappeared, and ahead was merely the chalk face of the cliff itself.

But of course, where there was a hill there was a chance of hill-lift, if the wind was blowing up it. Although when we had taken off the early morning wind was only a faint whisper, by now the land should have warmed up and the sea breeze begun to blow. There was also one more unknown. When a wind blows up a slope, it is quite certain to keep direct contact with the rising ground, and provide rising air near the slope even if one is flying half-way down it. But blowing against a vertical cliff the wind's behaviour is less certain. Sometimes lift can be found half-way down such a cliff, and near its face, but sometimes, in winds of certain strength, the air in the right-angle of the cliff and its base forms a rolling bolster, of which the side nearest the cliff face is actually moving downwards, and that furthest away slopes upwards, whilst over this upward-moving slope of air the main body of the wind climbs as if over a hill of gentler slope than the sheer cliff itself.

Each such cliff has its own particular characteristics in different wind-strengths and directions, but the trouble was that no one had ever before tried out this one. I certainly had no height to allow me to get it wrong the first time, and therefore had two chances to take: was there a wind, and if so was the upcurrent out from the cliff or near its face?

I was coming in at an angle of 30° to its line, so couldn't expect to fly through both possible locations of the upcurrent in a single straight dash.

I decided for the rock face itself, and about half-way down got my starboard wing well tucked into the chalk. Without hesitation the variometer swung to 'climb', and the fun was over. But not quite. After flying along the cliff-face, climbing rapidly, I cleared the top in about half a mile and went on up 1,000 feet to take a breath. I looked back to Worth, to see a line of dots hurrying across the field to the edge.

The workers of Worth, keenly conscious of their responsibility for my imagined plight, had dropped everything, rushed to the point at the cliff-top where I had last been seen, and were gadarening gallantly over the brow down towards the cruel sea below. They were, in their own line, undoubtedly the most brilliant scientists the world had seen, but they did not know that a sailplane could climb in an upcurrent of air. Directly over their heads the peaceful quiet in Minimoa's cockpit was disturbed by the odd chuckle.

The next day I was the Avro pilot, and my return to land was, for some reason, so delayed that when I made the coast my fuel was insufficient to get home, so I landed at R.A.F. Warmwell, with the petrol gauge at zero. For the last quarter of an hour all my faculties had been concentrated in an attempt to hypnotise my petrol-gauge into producing the last gallon of fuel needed to get me safely down. I taxied up to the control tower and went up to telephone Worth and tell them I would be late. The duty pilot gave me the phone, and I lifted it to ask for my number. No answer. I waggled the receiver several times, remarking acidly that, at such a time, the phone operators at a front-line operational station should be more on their toes. Suddenly an awful thought crossed my mind. I looked down at my 504 below. There, still attached to the tail, was the 300-foot towing cable which I had forgotten to drop before landing. Its trailing lower end had, as I crossed the aerodrome boundary, caught in the telephone wires and pulled down the whole lot. Warmwell was cut off from the outside world for over an hour.

After dinner in the Mess that evening came one of those personal and private big moments that no one else notices. Even at Worth, the staff had to eat and relax in talk, and I was sitting with two of the most inspiring men I met during the war, A. P. Rowe and Air Marshal Sir Philip Joubert. Our talk was of course of the war, and one of my companions turned to me and asked, 'What do you think of our chances of victory?' After a moment's thought I said 'About ten per cent, I should estimate. What do you think?' He looked for a moment at the end of his cigarette, then replied, quite calmly and judiciously, 'Oh, I wouldn't put it quite so high as *that*.'

The estimate of our chances of defeat and victory was a question of cold fact, to be judged as dispassionately as the latest figures of the power emission of the cavity magnetron, and of even more basic importance, since on it must be decided what proportion of the effort at Worth could be spared for long-range results, and how much confined to work calculated to produce immediate profit. We had to win the Battle of Britain, but after that we had to win the Battle of the Atlantic and, still further ahead, the re-conquest of Europe. If Worth had got the sum wrong and we lost the first, we lost everything. It was a nice calculation, to be made only by cool heads. And I had been asked, however casually, for my views, as a rational observer of facts, capable of isolating myself from the surcharged emotionalism of the times.

The day arrived when Worth was satisfied that they could detect gliders. But at that time our radiolocation stations only looked outwards, and could not keep track of an aircraft after it had crossed our coasts on its way inland. So it was important to find out if, after crossing our coastline, our ground-spotting system could be expected to track the expected visitors to their landing-points.

I was to be towed, climbing in a straight line, to 10,000 feet above Yeovil, where I was to release and fly straight back to Worth. The spotters were alerted, and for this first test given my exact course and times. The outcome was startling. Whilst on tow, the ground observers had no trouble in keeping track, but a minute after my release they lost me, on a fine clear summer's day, and did not pick me up again until down to 600 feet and preparing to land at Worth. It became quite clear that, to counter a glider-borne invasion effectively, an inward-looking radar chain was essential.

After this, my work at Worth was practically over. We produced a written report, which was delivered to the Air Ministry. The invasion scare had given momentum to the plan for a British glider-borne force, and I was asked if I would be prepared to transfer to it, but after some thought I declined. I have, perhaps, a too tidy mind, and like to see one job through: it seems to me so much more efficient not to chop and change around, leaving each job just as one has started to learn the essentials. Perhaps this is why I have stuck to gliding longer than most; certainly it is a subject which cannot be absorbed from beginning to end in one lifetime. So I returned to A.T.A., and never regretted it.

But the glider tests at Worth went on for some time longer. Slingsby made a special machine with practically no metal in it: wood and plastic took the place of control wires and so forth. But R.D.F. still picked it up. In mid August, Davie and Fender in a glider over Christchurch actually saw a Heinkel shot down into the sea. The day they left, there were three hundred plus aircraft on the screen: clearly it would have been overdoing it to add Minimoa and Viking.

Was it any use? . . .

I remember a horrifying picture coming to me, whilst reading some medical article on the onset of a virulent disease, of a small focus of the virus establishing itself in the body of a man; of the rapid multiplication and spread by compound interest, until quite rapidly every cell of the body is permeated with the poison; until the parasite kills the body it feeds on and so condemns itself to death by its very unthinking fecundity.

The position of *Homo sapiens* in the world today seems to me a parallel, man being the virus, the terrestrial globe the host. Geniuses like Lister and Fleming who, by the discovery of antiseptics and penicillin, have defeated the forces of nature which have previously put some limit to the rate of increase of mankind, before man has reached the stage of intelligence and co-operation necessary to enable him to adopt counterbalancing methods of population control, appear paradoxically to have shortened immeasurably the expectation of life of the species.

The world will remain habitable for millions of years, but man will have sucked dry its riches of metals, fuels, and even its soil, in a period to be measured in mere millennia; after which there seems no prospect but internecine warfare for the dying resources of the globe, followed by extinction, or at best a reversion for a tiny number to a life of the utmost primitive simplicity with no hope of betterment over the millions of years inexorably to come.

This sombre picture may seem to some defeatist, to others irrelevant or even ridiculous, an extrapolation to cloud-cuckoo-land. But to me it seems a prospect to be weighed up as dispassionately as our chances of victory or defeat in 1940. If one assumes that there is a very considerable chance of its accuracy, then the inference is that now – the last hundred and the next thousand years – is the golden age of man; with all its imperfections, this is our finest hour. Therefore our goal should be to make it as fine an hour as can possibly be created.

To switch from these cosmic considerations to the subject of soaring flight is, of course, to pass from the sublime almost to the ridiculous. Nevertheless, with the discovery of the art of true flying, without mechanical assistance, a tiny strand of an entirely new colour has been woven into the texture of living. The ever-increasing population brings with it remorselessly the necessity of ever-increasing regimentation. The corollary of mass population is mass production. Forms and schedules multiply almost as fast as men, and life itself becomes more fustian. The majority spend their lives on the 8.15, at work, home again, watching other people on the television, or other people playing games. More and more people get less and less experience of life at first hand.

The land is almost tamed, the sea only available to some. But the air is all around us, and although red tape has almost closed the door to the ordinary man, through gliding he can still find a way to the freedom of the sky, and a sport which, at his weekends, can give full scope to initiative, energy, intelligence, and the adventurous spirit.

It is not from any such laborious reasoning that I or my friends take up the art of soaring flight. But I think such considerations are sufficiently valid to enable one to suggest that those who wish to should be encouraged to do so.

2

WE CUT LOOSE

I started gliding in 1932, after owning a light aeroplane for two or three years, and finding this branch of aviation pall. The latent possibilities of motorless flight were at the time practically unrealised in England, although mysterious stories filtered through of remarkable flights in Germany. From downhill dashes in elementary gliders I graduated to hill soaring, and during a weekend meeting at Sutton Bank in Yorkshire made the headlines by flying along the range of hills and landing 12½ miles away from my starting-point. But this was small stuff, and one felt all the time the artificiality of flying limited to such special areas of country.

Then came 18th March 1934, and suddenly all the wonderland stories from Germany came true. The following description of what happened that day does not sound very impressive now, but at the time it seemed that a miracle had hit all three of the pilots who were able to take advantage of it.

To do a thing which has never been done before, however easy its repetition may subsequently become, is astonishingly more difficult than one may imagine. To remain airborne in 1932 above Dunstable Downs for five minutes, and so earn a 'C' certificate, earned loud and prolonged cheers from the club members watching from the top of the hill. And when I say 'earned' I mean it. The pilot was doing something which had only been done before by a

Lenticular cloud near Dunedin, New Zealand. The left edge is in the lee of a mountain; a strong wind is blowing left to right.

Wave clouds in Scotland.

handful of human beings since the beginning of time, and there was no body of comfortable experience behind him to tell him, before take-off, exactly what might happen during his flight and what counter-actions he might be called on to take.

The three of us who flew cross-country on that day were virtually plumbing the unknown, so far as pilots of this country were concerned. We were virgin, ecstatic and determined. It is something one can only be once.

On Sunday, 18th March 1934, I arrived at Dunstable rather late, about 12.30, but fortunately found the London Club 'Professor' still in the hangar, although the Red Wren, with Humphries, and the two-seater, with Collins and Exner, were already in the air.

A brisk north-west wind was blowing, and conditions looked good, so we hastily rigged the machine, and at the last moment I thought I would give my newly acquired recording barograph a first try-out, so took that along too.

By the time we got to the top of the hill the other two machines were specks in the distance under a beautiful street of clouds which had gone over about five minutes earlier, so, fizzing with impatience, I got into the cockpit and hastily stowed the barograph on the floor where it was just out of the way of my left foot. I was launched at 1.15, at about 1.40 the upcurrent of an advancing line of clouds took me violently in its grip, and at about 1,600 feet I cut loose from the hill and circled away with it.

About a mile upwind of me was a heavy storm of hail, and I used this as a signpost and endeavoured to keep my position a constant distance in front of it. The rate-of-climb indicator was not on this day fitted in the Professor, and so I am unable to say where or how violent were the upcurrents. The barograph record shows that they were of considerable strength, and I am nearly sure that there was actual lift inside the hailstorm, although this seems somewhat remarkable.

The first upcurrent carried me to about 3,800 feet (above sea-level) and at about this height I circled along for 15 or 20 miles, when the hailstorm caught me up, and I found myself flying blind inside it, even more blind because, in the open cockpit, it rapidly dimmed my spectacles; so I stopped circling and made a line out of it. I emerged on the south side, over a town which I subsequently identified as Welwyn, although being without a map at the time I was pretty well lost. Having lost the lift, I looked for a good field and circled round it, gradually descending to 1,800 feet.

I now struck a second upcurrent under another advancing cloud street, and rapidly climbed again to the highest point of the flight, 4,500 feet. Even now, the cloud base was still well above me, and I circled off again until I saw, south of me, the large reservoirs north of Enfield, which told me where I was. Then I spotted North Weald aerodrome, and as by this time I was very cold, I thought I would land there. But when, after about 20 minutes circling, in which to my disappointment I raised no sign of life on the aerodrome below, a third area of lift took me up to 3,700 feet I gave up the struggle to get down and went on again.

After North Weald the country is featureless, and without a map I was quite incapable of making a course, so simply went where I was taken. A couple of Moths came up from behind me, 2,000 feet below, and passed directly underneath without seeing me. I read the markings of one – G-EBVK – on its wings, which was a joyous moment. Both pilots evidently had their eyes glued inside the office; the Professor after all had more than twice their span and must nearly have filled the meagre arc of vision which a biplane offers above the pilot.

A surprisingly short time afterwards, I began to see water coming at me from all sides. Had I had a map, I could have gone a few miles north and then have carried on east a deal further, but by now I had ceased to feel competitive – only cold – so at what seemed the last sizeable town before the coast (later identified as Maldon) I started circling down from about 2,000 feet. When I got lower I saw a village a little further east that gave promise of connection with the outside world, so went on to that.

I landed in a field of low blackberry bushes, which luckily proved quite harmless: two and a half hours after my launch and 55 miles away.

I proved extremely fortunate in my choice of a landing place. A quarter of a mile away, in the village of Latchingdon, the *Waggon and Horses* produced everything necessary for both pilot and machine – including a miraculous shed which exactly took the dismantled Professor.

Five minutes later I was on the telephone, and ten more and my wife was talking to me from Hatfield, where she had chased me in our baby car and finally lost me.

And so back to the field, where I found the village assembled, and promptly put them all to work dismantling the machine. Then we set off, a wonderful procession. Two men and I came first, carrying the fuselage, then a collection of boys and girls carrying the rudder and elevators, then a couple of men with one wing, a man and a woman with the centre section, two stout-hearted girls with the other wing, and the cavalcade brought up in the rear by two diminutive children carrying the wing struts. We straggled in a long column out of the field and along the road to the pub, stowed the bits carefully in the shed, and then thankfully repaired to the bar. Finally, with my precious barograph under my arm, I came home in a state of huge elation and the slowest train it has ever been my misfortune to accompany.

The flight just described was my first successful thermal cross-country flight: with it I won the British single-seater distance and height records.

The Professor was an early German high-performance design. By modern standards, the controllability of this machine left much to be desired. Aileron drag was so formidable that I can remember doing a full left-hand circle with full right-hand aileron and rudder applied; whilst the fore-and-aft trim was such that once, when I let go of the stick for a moment to grab an errant map, the machine made a stout effort to do a forward loop so violently that, but for the seat-belt, I might have been thrown out of the cockpit.

The only instrument fitted on the day of the flight was an air-speed indicator, and even this was considered, in those days, to be rather an effeminate device. In addition I carried a kind of pocket altimeter strapped to my wrist. I also carried, for the first time, a recording barograph. I had no map, and this remains the only cross-country flight I have ever achieved without a rate-of-climb indicator. David Dent had just invented his ingenious instrument, which shortly afterwards came into use, consisting of concentric glass tubes filled with two solutions of carbolic acid. It was only too easy to spill the liquids out, and I will never forget the taste, as one hurriedly attempted to refill it by sucking phenol up in a pipette which then had to be probed into the glass intestines of the instrument. It must indeed have been a day of strong upcurrents, to have enabled the three of us to keep going so long without this, the basic instrument of all soaring flights.

On this same day, Eric Collins got within a few miles of the world two-seater distance record by flying the London Club's Kassel two-seater 45 miles from Dunstable to Little Waltham. Collins was one of the only two 'natural' pilots I have known in the British gliding world. (Squadron-Leader Willy Watt, killed in the first week of the war, was the other.) If Collins had lived, we should, I feel certain, not have had to wait till 1952 to reach the front rank in motorless flight.

Collins's flight on this day, with mine and a third by Sebert Humphries of 19 miles, did I think signal the emergence of the British gliding movement from its ground-hopping and hill-bound days, and virtually we never looked back, though development was naturally quicker at some times than others. Before this day, some people held that the thermal and cloud-soaring performances of the Germans were not possible in England, because of our inferior weather conditions. But when three British pilots in one day showed that this was fallacious, everyone else started to try and it was not long before cross-country flying ceased to be regarded as a cross between a conjuring trick and plain magic.

3

FLIGHT WITHOUT POWER

For the benefit of the newcomer, let me now revert to fairly elementary matters. How does a glider stay up without an engine? The answer is that, *relative to the air*, it doesn't, it is always descending. Launch a paper glider across a room, and it flies forwards, descending at a constant angle. Trim it to fly faster, and it descends more rapidly. The same thing happens with any unpowered heavier-than-air aircraft.

An intermediate sailplane, as an example, may lose height at a rate of $2\frac{1}{2}$ feet per second flying at 30 m.p.h., or 44 ft./sec.; this roughly equals losing one foot in seventeen, which means that in still air flying at 30 m.p.h. the glider is descending an invisible slope of 1 in 17.

If however the pilot of the sailplane can find a region where the air is rising at $2\frac{1}{2}$ ft./sec., clearly he will hold his height, and in a region of air rising faster than this he will climb. If, having found such an area of rising air, he manœuvres his aircraft so as to stay within it, he will climb in the aerial fountain until he reaches the altitude near its summit where its rate of ascent has fallen off to the figure of $2\frac{1}{2}$ ft./sec. He is now in the position of a man walking down a moving stairway at the same speed as it is rising.

There are three main kinds of aerial fountains, each by their nature calling for a different kind of manœuvre. The first two kinds are commonly used by soaring birds, and the sailplane pilot copies their tactics as exactly as he can.

Orographic Lift. This type of upcurrent is the simplest to understand. It is caused when a surface wind meets a line of hills across its path. Clearly the air has to rise to get over the top of the hill. Figure 1 shows the sort of things which happen in various different circumstances. The glider pilot flying in this kind of upcurrent copies exactly the gull flying off the cliffs in an on-shore breeze. He tacks to and fro, keeping roughly over the crest of the slope below him.

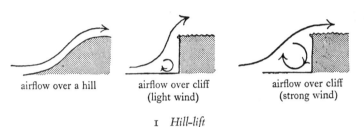

airflow over a hill   airflow over cliff   airflow over cliff
                            (light wind)   (strong wind)

1   *Hill-lift*

Since few hills are of constant height or run in an exactly straight line, he has to learn how the upcurrent is affected by bays or knolls, and by the wind blowing obliquely to the hill instead of directly up it. Every hill possesses its own special characteristics in this respect. Since in England the prevailing winds blow from the west, a gliding club tries to establish itself on a westerly facing slope which will provide hill-soaring conditions on the maximum number of days. Examples are the London Gliding Club at Dunstable, the Midland Club at the Long Mynd, the Derby and Lancs Club at Camphill, the Yorkshire Club at Sutton Bank, and the Scottish Gliding Union at Bishop Hill.

The great virtue of hill soaring is that upcurrents are to be found all the year round, whenever the winds blow from the right quarter. Thus flights of great duration can be made in any part of the world where steady winds blow for long periods up a hill. The length of time one can stay up is then limited only by the physical endurance of the pilot: the present world duration record exceeds 50 hours. Flights of great height or distance, however, cannot be made by simple hill-lift. The other two methods of soaring are much more seasonally restricted, but on the other hand much more interesting and dramatic flights can be achieved through them.

Hill-lift can be used by a glider pilot to keep himself airborne until he can find thermal lift, which enables him to sever his invisible bonds and circle away across country.

Thermal Lift. To understand thermal upcurrents, remember two things. A balloon full of hot air rises, because hot air is lighter than cold air. This is because when you heat air (or anything else) it expands. So a balloon full of hot air contains less air than a balloon of the same size full of cold air. Thus it weighs less than the air it displaces, and like a cork under water, which weighs less than the water it displaces, it will tend to rise.

The second point to remember is that, if you breathe warm moist air on to a cold window-pane, a film of moisture will condense on to the glass, because your breath, when cold, cannot hold as much water-vapour as when warm.

Now visualise the sun shining on a small island in the sea. The dry land gets hotter than the surrounding water, so the air above it becomes warmer than the air over the sea, expands and starts to rise. The sea air blows in from all round to take its place, creating the shallow on-shore sea breeze which is a common experience for all who go to the seaside.

The pressure of the air above us is, at sea-level, the startling figure of nearly 15 lb. per square inch or nearly one ton per

40

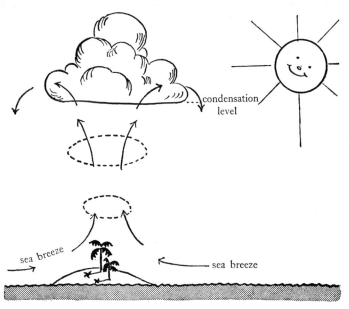

2 *Thermal upcurrent*

square foot. As one climbs up towards the surface of the ocean of air, the pressure obviously decreases. At 20,000 feet it has come down to half the figure at ground-level. A closed balloon full of hydrogen will distend more and more as it climbs, owing to the reducing pressure outside, until finally it will burst just as a deep-sea fish will burst if brought too rapidly to the surface. A column or bubble of hot air rising from our island will not burst, since it is not restricted by any envelope, but will expand. As a gas expands, it becomes cooler: because it has to do mechanical work by forcing its surroundings away from it to make room for it. When a gas is compressed, it gets hotter for the reverse reason: the valve of a bicycle tyre is heated when you pump the tyre up.

41

Thus as the thermal rises, the air in it cools, and it always cools at the same rate, called the *adiabatic lapse rate*. But the general body of air in the surrounding atmosphere also gets colder as one climbs, hence snow-topped mountains. This rate of cooling is not, however, always the same. If the rate of cooling of the surrounding air is less than that of the rising thermal, the air in the thermal will quickly cool down to the same temperature as that of the air around it, and will cease to rise. If the surrounding air cools at the same rate (adiabatic) the thermal will continue to rise steadily. If the surrounding air cools even more rapidly than the rising air, the thermal's rate of ascent will increase, because, relative to the surrounding air, as it rises it is getting even hotter. In such super-adiabatic conditions the atmosphere is called unstable. The passenger in an airliner calls it bumpy (or worse); the glider pilot thanks nature for her gift, for on such a day he is free of the air.

The rising, cooling thermal will eventually reach a temperature at which it can no longer hold within it its water-content as a gas. At this level the water-vapour condenses and forms a cloud, just as the moisture in your breath condenses on the cold window-pane.

Now a somewhat odd physical law comes into play. If you heat a beaker-full of water from freezing to boiling point, you then have to put in over five times as much heat again to turn the whole of the water into steam. In reverse, when steam at 100° C. condenses to water at 100° C., a large amount of heat is released. This concealed packet of heat is called *latent heat*; the phenomenon is called the *latent heat of condensation*.

When the water-vapour in a thermal condenses and forms a cloud, it gives off heat. This is not enough actually to increase the temperature of the air in the cloud, but it reduces the rate at which it cools as it rises. All other things being equal, a cloud therefore tends to grow higher of its own volition, and the glider climbing in an upcurrent frequently finds his rate of climb increases once he climbs into the cloud which caps it.

The kind of cloud capping the ordinary thermal is the 'wool-pack' or cumulus cloud, which looks exactly like what it is, the visible top of an invisible aerial fountain. When atmospheric conditions are suitable, cumulus clouds, by the release of latent heat, grow into the gigantic storm-clouds called cumulo-nimbus. Such clouds can grow higher than 30,000 feet, producing rain, hail, lightning and similar delights, and upcurrents of 30 or 40 ft./sec. inside are not unusual. Aeroplane pilots don't like them. Sailplane pilots, properly equipped with modern aircraft and instruments and the knowledge of what is likely to be going on inside it, and why, regard a carefully selected cumulo-nimbus (one with its base well above the ground, and of not too great horizontal extent) as a big-game fisherman regards the approach of a gigantic fish.

Finally, some dull figures. Adiabatic lapse rate (the fall of temperature of a body of air expanding as it rises through the atmosphere): 5.6° F. per 1,000 ft. in clear air; 3° F. per 1,000 ft. in saturated air (*i.e.* in cloud). Send up a met. balloon with a thermometer, and record the reading of the thermometer every 1,000 ft. If it records a temperature drop in clear air of less than 5.6° F. per 1,000 ft., the air is *stable*: thermal currents starting to rise from hot ground will rapidly be damped out. The technical term for this is that the temperature gradient, or lapse rate, is sub-adiabatic. If the balloon's thermometer, however, shows that in the general atmosphere the lapse rate is greater than 5.6° F. per 1,000 ft. the air is unstable, and if the instability goes high enough there will be numerous thermal upcurrents over the land, with cumulus and possibly cumulo-nimbus clouds capping them.

The manœuvre for keeping within the rising column of a thermal is again identical with that used by soaring birds, notably by birds such as vultures: find your thermal, then circle within it, drifting along with the wind as you circle. Thus you fly in correct air-circles, not in circles round a stationary point on the ground.

On a cross-country flight the sailplane pilot circles up in his thermal as high as he can, or wants to climb, then straightens out and flies in the direction he wishes to go. His problem is to find more lift on the way, in which he again gains height by circling. With experience he learns the likely sort of country over which he may expect to find lift, or the kinds of clouds under which upcurrents are to be found, and makes his course accordingly. The present world record distance flight made in this way is 545 miles (Richard Johnson, U.S.A., in an R.J.5, Odessa-Salina, Kansas, 5th August 1951).

Since thermals are created by the sun, they are much more frequent and larger in the warmer months of the year.

Waves. Wave-lift is the latest kind of upcurrent discovered by the glider pilot, and also possibly the most difficult kind to understand. It occurs, oddly enough, in conditions in some respects opposite to those producing either hill-lift or thermal lift: when a torrent of *stable* air blows *down* a line of hills or range of mountains. It is, like hill-lift, a more or less stationary upcurrent in relation to the ground, as opposed to the thermal upcurrent which drifts along with

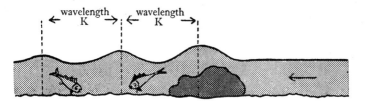

3   *Standing waves in water*

the wind; and also the opposite of thermal in that it forms in stable air instead of unstable air.

Some kind of a parallel may be seen in a fast-flowing river. A large totally submerged boulder will cause a hump in the surface of the water above it. But downstream of this hump the water will hump itself up again into one or sometimes more secondary waves, stationary in relation to each other and to the banks of the river, with the water itself flowing through them. It there are more than one of these standing waves, it can be seen that the distance between the crest of the first and second is always the same as the distance between the second, third and following crests. In other words, the wavelength is constant.

A torrent of stable air blowing across a range of mountains will, because it is stable, behave much like water in that it will pour down the lee side and create one or more standing waves downstream of the foot of the mountains. But the height of the water wave is limited by the height of the general surface of the stream itself: by the discontinuity between the water and the air above it. The air wave has no such limiting ceiling and the wave starting in air near ground-level may imprint itself on the air above it to quite startling altitudes. Standing waves have carried a two-seater sailplane to the extraordinary height of the present world absolute altitude record, 44,500 feet (Edgar and Klieforth, U.S.A., Bishop, California), whence the pilot had to descend because above that altitude it is impossible to live on oxygen alone. When a pressure-cabin sailplane is built, it is expected to find that the Bishop wave ascends in suitable conditions to altitudes in excess of 60,000 feet.

A standing wave in the air may repeat itself downstream a considerable number of times at regular intervals, each successive wave being a little lower than the one before. In the right conditions, the crest of each layer of a wave is marked by a very typical lens-shaped cloud, called a lenticular cloud, or 'eyebrow'. This cloud is stationary in relation to the ground, and when flying near it in a sailplane the effect is of a silent racing torrent of dazzling white foam, appearing from thin air at the front or upwind edge, sweeping up and over like a surf wave at sea, and rushing down to disappear mysteriously along the back, downwind edge. A wave upcurrent is quite extraordinarily smooth, and only by watching his variometer can the pilot realise that he is climbing. The spectacle of a wave cloud, observed in the utter silence of a wave flight in a sailplane, is one of the unique experiences to which the sailplane pilot alone is privileged.

In a big wave system, wave clouds can occur at several levels at the same time, and a sailplane can climb far above a lenticular. The technique of wave flying is the opposite to that for thermal flying. The object is, roughly speaking, after locating the wave, to stay as nearly as possible stationary in relation to the *ground*, and as most wave clouds are formed in high winds, this is achieved by pointing the sailplane into wind and flying just fast enough to 'stay put' over the ground below.

Waves in England are found over some of our hill-sites, notably the Long Mynd and Camphill. The largest British wave so far explored, and that only once, is at Hartside in Cumberland, where the phenomena accompanying it have been noticed from the earliest times. The north-east wind creating it is called the Helm Wind, the lower stationary roll cloud formed by this wind is called the Helm Bar, the lenticulars above it the High Bars. The Helm, or Cap, is a helmet of cloud on top of the ridge, out of which the Helm Wind appears to pour.

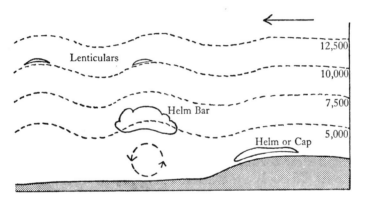

4   *The Helm Wind*

Numerous other systems of wave clouds have been observed in Great Britain and Northern Ireland, notably in various parts of Scotland, over the vale of Thirsk east of the Pennines in a west wind, and even over the Isle of Wight. But the highest ones are likely to be found in the lee of large mountain ranges, such as the Bishop wave which occurs in the lee of the Sierra Nevada in California, or a large and only slightly explored system which the Germans called the

Alpine Wall, occurring when the southerly Foehn wind blows over the Alps. There are also probably systems of the largest dimensions created by the main mountain range in the South Island of New Zealand, in Norway, Iceland and elsewhere. In these incredibly remote regions of the upper air lie possibly the last mysteries of the atmosphere and in the glider we have probably the best instrument with which to explore them.

Dynamic Lift. I now come to the one field of soaring in which the birds still outclass us, and alas, I can see little prospect of the human bird ever being able to compete.

Anyone who has, from the deck of a steamer, watched an albatross circling for hours over the wave crests with motionless wings, has seen an exhibition of dynamic soaring which is as beautiful a vision of instinctive skill and poetic, effortless grace as can be seen in the whole world of nature. Whence comes the supply of power used by the albatross to keep aloft in this way?

The albatross keeps to those parts of the globe where winds blow continuously. When a fresh wind blows over the sea, lift can be extracted from it in two ways. The first is from the shifting upcurrents created by the air blowing over the waves of the sea itself, producing an immensely complicated variation of simple hill-lift.

The second way is by using the '*wind-gradient*'. The wind at the actual surface of the sea will be slowed down by friction, so that a wind-strength of, say, 20 knots at 50 feet may only be 10 knots at the surface. Close observation of the soaring albatross will show that his flight-path is ideally as follows.

The evolution starts by gliding *into wind* at the surface of the sea. He then climbs, flying straight ahead, to from 25 to

An eagle shares an upcurrent with a sailplane over the Pyrenees.

The old (top) and new way of building a glider. When the author was World Champion gliders were made of plywood, now they are built of moulded resin-bonded fibreglass.

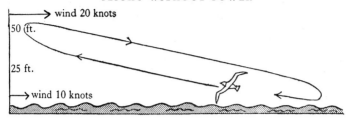

5 *Dynamic soaring in wind-gradient*

50 feet above it, then turns 180° and descends *downwind* until, back near the surface again, he again turns into wind and starts his climb once more.

This is the correct theoretical evolution for dynamic soaring in the surface wind-gradient, but in practice it is usually varied at any moment by the bird darting off at a tangent to make use of 'hill-lift' along the line of some adjacent wave.

Analysing the dynamics of this evolution, let us assume that the bird's most efficient air-speed is 30 knots, and assume also a surface wind of 10 knots increasing to 20 knots at 50 feet. At sea-level, flying into a 10-knot wind, the bird is covering the 'ground' at 20 knots. Now he starts to climb, and his ground-speed falls off: but as he is climbing into a continually increasing wind, he can retain his optimum air-speed with an increment which he can turn into height. When he reaches the level at which the wind-gradient falls off, he turns downwind and starts to descend (at 50 knots ground-speed, but still 30 knots flying-speed) into the increasingly slower air-stream below. Keeping a steady air-speed, his ground-speed will lessen as he gets lower, and again there will be an increment which he can either use to flatten his glide or to pick up more air-speed to turn into height when he again, just over the water, swoops round into wind preparatory to another climb.

This description will indicate the grounds for my pessimism: for both these kinds of lift are only available between the actual surface of the sea and a height of, say, 50 feet above it. A man-carrying sailplane, with a wing-span even as low as 30 feet, would be on too big a scale to be able to operate in such a shallow layer of air; and without the instant source of emergency power so unfairly possessed by the sea-bird, who can flap, the first miscalculation must bring disaster.

I know I am running the risk of being thought 'precious' in what I am about to say. Yet I can shut my eyes and feel myself soaring in this way, for hours and days and nights over the restless sea. The clean and steadily increasing pressure of the air in the climb; the free and ecstatic wheel downwind; the exhilaration of the fast dive back to the surface; then a quick flexion of the wings and round again facing the incessant wind and the broken white-capped surface of the ocean, at eye-level, to the near horizon.

The yachtsman must get a faint echo of the first climbing surge from the tug of his sheet when a gust strikes his sails. Somewhere in our line of ancestors, back to the primeval seas, we come to the point when the spur of the birds-to-be branched off. Can instinct run dimly back down the tree of life and then forwards down another branch? Certainly our dreams sometimes make it seem so: for we dream of flying like a bird, not in a clumsy machine.

Or perhaps I am just being precious – have it your own way. Anyway it is a shadow in the past, and I do not believe we shall ever be able to repeat it.

I do want to ram home as clearly as I can the extraordinarily wide range of moods of the air. The differences between the behaviour of stable and unstable air are such that it is hard to believe they are composed of the same elements.

Stable air is generally heavy, dead and lifeless. If you disturb it, as soon as you stop it tries to flop back to where it started from, like a dead fish on a fishmonger's slab.

Perhaps the best idea of its nature can be gathered from an occasion when it becomes visible. Flat river valleys on autumnal evenings often produce low streamers and fields of white, stationary mist. Sometimes one can walk through this up to the waist, able to see for miles, but unable to see one's feet. If a giant were to arrive with a pudding-spoon and stir it up, one can imagine that, immediately he stopped, the scraps of mist which he had been able to whisk up away from the ground would flop back and reform the shroud-like sheet on the meadow floor.

The contrast with unstable air is absolutely remarkable, for unstable air behaves like a slow-speed explosive: there being so vast a volume of it, the amount of power packed into a mass of unstable air can be almost inconceivable.

Imagine an absolutely flat and featureless desert, with no wind. The sun has heated the ground, which in turn has heated the layer of surface air until it is uniformly hotter than the air above it. Thus, a mass of millions of tons of hot, light surface air is trying to rise up, all at once, through the colder air above it. *It cannot do so*: if it did, it would leave a vacuum below it. Something has got to start a small bit of it rising, creating a pocket on the surface into which the cold air above can descend.

A rather similar situation would be a round lake on to which was placed a close-fitting disc of lead. The lead could not sink until a hole was drilled through it somewhere, through which the underlying water could pass to the top.

In our theoretical desert, a man lighting a theoretical match would create a tiny bubble of even hotter air which would break the impasse. The simile of a man lighting the fuse of a powder-mine is irresistible; for once the system has been set off, millions of horsepower will be released, and the surface air will start forming into rising columns or bubbles surrounded by areas of downcurrents. If the rising columns went high enough, they would form cumulo-nimbus clouds, thunderstorms, cloudbursts, or any of the violences of which unstable air is capable. Thus a match could theoretically set off a cloudburst.

There is some evidence to show that, on unstable days, the stirring up of the air over a gliding field occasioned by the winch-launching of a sailplane may set off a thermal up-current which may rise for thousands of feet and develop tens of thousands of horsepower, for on certain days the number of pilots who, after release, find themselves actually in rising air seems greater than can be accounted for other-wise.

The spectrum of this aspect of the air's character thus ranges from the infra-red of a treaclish stability through all intermediate shades to the ultra-violet of almost explosive instability.

What other dimensions has the character of the air? Well, first and foremost, the aspect that beyond any other eats its way into your bones, is that it is *big*.

This is so small a word, and one so over-used in these days of the cinematograph and of advertising that it seems inadequate to describe the air. The air is so big that nothing this side of astronomy can compare with it. It covers the whole surface of the globe, land and water, and unlike them it has no defined surface: it goes on indefinitely upwards growing imperceptibly rarer, but there is no precise level at which one could say one had reached the end of it.

Yet within itself it contains various mysterious boundaries. I have flown on a day when the upcurrents reached the top of a haze-level at four thousand feet, above which the sky was crystal clear; and porpoised silently and for hours in and out of the surface of a pale brown sea with wave crests five miles apart.

The air disposes of immense, almost incalculable power. A tiny fraction of it can pick up a million tons of fresh water out of the South Atlantic and drop them a few weeks later five thousand miles away on the British Isles.

What else can one say of it? It weighs a ton for every square foot of the surface of the globe. It has no colour and every colour – invisible yet able to become visible, and when it does so, appearing in every shade and colour of the visible spectrum.

But I come back to where I started : it is big. It gives you a sense of proportion. Which is badly needed in the mid-twentieth century.

In October 1936 I went to South Africa on a business trip, and took the opportunity of taking with me a Kirby Kite sailplane. At that time one or two gliding clubs had started in the Union, but no one had yet made contact with thermal lift, and consequently no cross-country or altitude flights had been made.

Just as had happened in England five years before, there were folk who said that high-performance soaring was not possible on the high veld, owing to the altitude, which runs between 4,000 feet and 6,000 feet above sea-level. No one asked these critics to look up at the vultures and other soaring birds wheeling silently, for hours on end, over their heads.

It was not long before the spell was broken by my doing a goal flight of 32 miles from the site of the Rand Gliding Club to the civil airport at Germiston, Johannesburg. But the most interesting discovery of the trip, made I believe for the first time, was How the Vultures Do It.

We all know the scene, I think. The caravan toiling across the empty desert, under the brilliant, hot and dusty sky. The flagging horses (or camels, if the book is by E. M. Dell). Eventually one animal stumbles and falls, too weak to continue. It is left behind. Almost at once, from nowhere, in the sky overhead appears a small black dot. It descends rapidly, and lands near the dying animal: a vulture with a meal in sight. Rapidly other dots appear overhead and scream down. In a few minutes the still dying animal is being torn to pieces by the hooked beaks of a host of shrieking carrion birds.

How did they get there?

The Rand Gliding Club was established on a rough field at the foot of a rocky range of north-facing low hills at Quaggapoort, near Pretoria, about 5,000 feet above sea-level. From the top of the hills, looking south, were miles of almost flat brownish-green veld country. In October, the end of the dry season, everything was dusty and dry. The nights in the club's wooden hut were freezingly cold, but by day a hard blue sky brought the temperature up to near the nineties.

Manhandling the glider up this slope in the sun was a tough task, but once at the top, the wind blew persistently and every day from the north, so hill-lift was regularly available. One was catapulted off by the cheery club members, and turned and climbed along the crest of the hill below. It might not be until after some hours in the morning air that the mounting sun would set off the first thermal. Then there would be a surge, the green ball of the rate-of-climb indicator would jump up, and one would set the machine into a climbing circle.

Almost invariably, after a very short time a large brownish-white bird would appear, flying rapidly towards the glider. When it entered the thermal it also would start to circle, with wings motionless. Shortly afterwards other similar shapes would appear, and soon the Kite would be just one of a large flock of silently circling birds.

Frequently one or other bird would come to within a few feet of me, so close that I could see his steady unwinking eye. I observed how, in the air, the long scraggy neck of these birds is retracted into the body, leaving a perfectly streamlined shape. There could be no question of it: I was accepted by the vultures as just an unexpectedly large brother.

To a glider pilot, the explanation of all this was blindingly obvious. The scene dissolves into the green slopes of Dunstable Downs, five thousand miles away, with half a dozen sailplanes soaring to and fro along the line of the hill. Suddenly one of the pilots, encountering a thermal, puts his machine into a circle. Instantly all the others, scattered along the slope and seeing the manœuvre of the lucky one, turn and flock towards him. As they enter the area of rising air, they too start to circle, and together the flock of aircraft screw themselves silently up into the sky.

To any glider pilot, the sight of a bird circling is an infallible sign of lift, of which he immediately takes advantage by flying over and joining the bird. In South Africa, here were the vultures returning the compliment. Indeed, when I came to think of it, why should they not? In the air, they have no enemies.

As time went on, and this experience recurred again and again, I started to consider it more closely. I found that, as it happened, the flying speed of the birds was almost exactly the same as my own: about 30 m.p.h. I next checked the average time between my first starting a circle and the arrival of the first visitor: it was a fairly constant 60 seconds. Furthermore, I noted that almost invariably my wheeling companions would desert me at about 2,500 feet above the ground, after which I would continue my climb alone.

The next point which struck me was that the bird which first arrived, after a lapse of one minute, flying at 30 m.p.h., would have come a distance of half a mile – or 2,500 feet – which was the same distance as the height above ground at which the flock would abandon me. With these data, the operational tactics of the vulture became clear. Let us first analyse his problem.

The vulture is a large and heavy bird, and a meat-eater. The only way he can find his food is by keeping on the wing for as long as possible every day, scanning the ground below. The energy required to keep so heavy a body aloft for hours on end, by means of flapping flight, would be altogether too great, and would put up his required intake of fuel to an unacceptable degree. Therefore the solution is to keep aloft by soaring effortlessly in upcurrents.

But to find the largest number of upcurrents, searching the sky at random, involves flying as fast as possible. The necessary shape for fast flying allied to efficient soaring is that of the albatross – a long thin wing with what is termed a high aspect-ratio, that is, a large span in relation to its chord

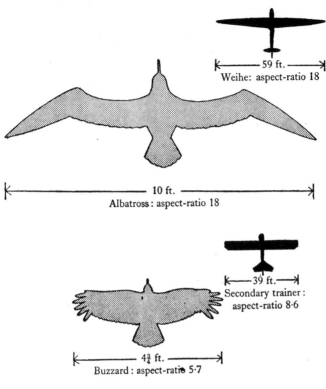

59 ft.
Weihe: aspect-ratio 18

10 ft.
Albatross: aspect-ratio 18

39 ft.
Secondary trainer:
aspect-ratio 8·6

4¾ ft.
Buzzard: aspect-ratio 5·7

6   *Aspect-ratio*

and a high wing-loading, which is defined as the weight per square foot of wing area. Such a wing only provides lift at relatively high air-speeds, and this is why the albatross is only found in regions of the globe where fairly strong winds blow constantly, such as the 'Roaring Forties'. An albatross can only take off by paddling and flapping for a long distance, as hard as he can, into wind, during which take-off run he gradually achieves the minimum air-speed needed to become airborne. If a captured albatross is put down on the deck of a steamer, or on a lake in calm air, it is helpless.

The vulture, however, lives on land, and in climates hot enough to produce the constant thermal upcurrents he needs for his daily hunt for food. Such climates are relatively wind-less, hence he must have a low-speed take-off, involving a wing of low aspect-ratio, low wing-loading, and compara-tively low flying-speed characteristics. Thus he cannot expect to find enough thermals simply by darting around and covering a great deal of air in his search. And even Nature has found no way of sensing invisible columns of rising air from afar off.

My experience pointed to the solution: and once again it was the solution which had been arrived at independently by the soaring pilot. The vultures form a co-operative society.

Imagine the whole sky of Africa covered by a gigantic invisible fisherman's net, tossed into the air. Each knot is represented by a searching vulture – searching for two things, lift and food. Each bird flies within sight of his neighbours, and watches both them and the ground beneath. There are two signals, and only two.

One bird finds an upcurrent, which it probably detects by 'hearing' it. The ear of a bird is constructed in the reverse way to that of a man. Increasing air-pressure stretches the human eardrum, and thus causes an uncomfortable feeling, or even actual pain, in a steep dive. Much less sensation is felt in decreasing pressure, that is in a climb. The bird's eardrum is anchored from the opposite side, so is stretched by *de-creasing* pressure, thus in all likelihood giving him a sensa-tion when he climbs.

Immediately this vulture 'hears' his upcurrent, he starts to circle, and instantly on this signal his neighbours fly in towards him and join in, whilst in turn, by chain reaction, *their* neighbours do likewise. Soon this part of the sky presents the familiar scene of a host of birds wheeling up silently together on motionless wings. At a given height, when they have reached the limit of their range of vision beyond which they could not see that which they are searching for below, they have extracted all the benefit they can get from their upcurrent, and return silently to their previous stations. This height was clearly half a mile – and clearly therefore, since they must also keep within sight of each other, their aerial sentry beats must also be within half a mile of each other – the mesh of the imaginary net must be of this order of size. This point also seemed to be proven by my observation of the time interval between my starting a circle and the arrival of the first bird to join me: time for him to travel half a mile.

When one bird sees a prospective kill below, he folds his wings and plummets downwards. At this, the second signal, again the neighbours dash inwards, followed by their neighbours in turn.

I need hardly say that this was an evolution I was unable to try out for myself in the same way, but there can, I think, be no doubt that this is the correct solution. And it is interesting to reflect that it was reached, not by the ornithologist, but by the sailplane pilot, as an entirely unexpected by-product of his normal activities.

4

A FEW SQUARE FEET OF PLYWOOD

It is time to have a look at the aircraft themselves. The first thing to examine is what we want of them. We need, first, a class of machine on which to train pilots. This type of aircraft must clearly be safe and easy to fly, with viceless aerodynamic and handling characteristics, and both rugged and cheap to make and to repair.

Secondly, we need a class of aircraft for advanced flying, after the preliminary training period has been completed. In this class, good performance – *i.e.* efficiency – becomes an additional requirement, and unfortunately this is antipathetic to cheapness and repairability, and to some degree to ease of pilotage. To discuss this problem, it is necessary to go more deeply into the meaning of the words 'good performance', and to explain some of the major terms we shall have to use.

Sinking Speed. This is the rate at which height is lost by the glider as it flies forwards. If one puts down the nose of the glider, it will, of course, fly faster. At a given forward speed, as a rule fairly near its minimum flying speed (stalling speed), sinking speed will be at a minimum.

If one flies either faster or slower than this *minimum sinking speed*, the machine will lose height faster.

Gliding Angle (sometimes called, more accurately, Glide Ratio). If the machine, in flying forwards say 20 feet at a given speed, loses one foot of height, its gliding angle is 1 in 20. It can be shown that this angle is the same as the inverse proportion of Lift divided by Drag (or L/D) at any given speed. It is common, therefore, to say of such an aircraft that at this given speed its 'L over D' is 20. Its best gliding angle (or max. L/D) will be achieved at a speed somewhat greater than its minimum sinking speed. (Figures 7 and 8.)

Polar Curve. The polar curve of a glider is the graph showing its sinking speed at different flying speeds. (See Figure 7.)

Penetration Curve. The penetration curve shows graphically the aircraft's gliding angle at different flying speeds. (See Figure 8.)

Penetration. 'Penetration' is a word used by sailplane pilots to describe the capacity of a machine to get from one area of lift, through intervening calm or descending air, with maximum speed for a minimum loss of height. Figure 8 shows how, although the minimum sink of an elementary glider is only about three times that of an advanced sailplane, at 80 m.p.h. the elementary machine is diving vertically, making no ground at all, whilst the advanced sailplane is only losing height at $6\frac{1}{2}$ feet a second, and gliding at an angle of 1 in 15. The elementary aircraft has poor penetration, the advanced sailplane good penetration. Future advances in the design of sailplanes are likely to produce greater improvement in penetration than in any other quality.

Angle of Attack (or Angle of Incidence). This is the angle of the wing relative to the air-stream in which it is flying. (See Figure 9.) The angle of attack increases as speed decreases, and a given wing-section will stall at a certain fixed angle of attack.

Stalling Speed. An inherent characteristic of any aerofoil is that at a certain minimum speed the angle of attack rises to a

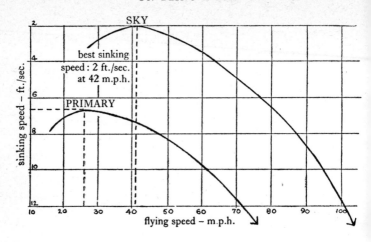

7 *Polar curve*

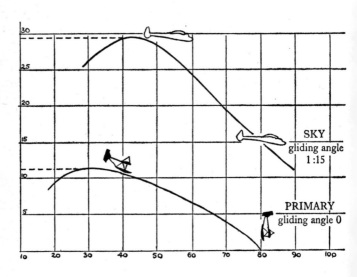

8 *Penetration curve*

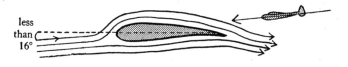

airflow – normal flight

airflow over stalled wing

9 *Angle of incidence*

point where the smooth flow of air over the upper surface of the wing suddenly breaks down, with consequent loss of control. This is the stalling speed. After stalling, control can only be regained by gaining speed through loss of height, and accordingly a stall must not be permitted low down.

The stalling speed of an aircraft varies with the load on the wing, thus an aircraft with a heavy man on board will stall at a slightly higher speed than with a light one, and stalling speed will increase sharply in a steep turn, when the wing-loading is increased by centrifugal force. (Whirl a stone round on the end of a string: the faster you whirl the heavier the stone appears to become.)

Oddly enough, however, increased weight does not affect the best gliding angle (max. L/D) of a machine, but this is then achieved at a higher forward speed. Minimum sinking speed is, of course, adversely affected by increased weight.

Aspect-Ratio. This has already been described on page 57.

Wing Taper. The easiest and cheapest wing to construct is obviously one of rectangular plan-form. Each rib of such a wing is the same shape, and hence can be subject to some degree of quantity production. Such a wing is also easily covered (or 'skinned') with plywood or fabric. Unfortunately a rectangular wing-shape is aerodynamically and structurally inefficient.

The strutted rectangular plan-form is thus employed on the simpler training aircraft, but in advanced aircraft wings of high aspect-ratio and a considerably tapered plan-form are necessary (Figure 6, p. 57). Strutted wings also obviously involve increased wind-resistance, or drag, so high-performance aircraft have to pay the penalty in price and weight and incorporate cantilever wings.

Wash-out. Imagine yourself standing at the end of a flexible wing, looking inwards towards the fuselage. Now twist the wing-tip by depressing its leading edge and lifting its trailing edge. By this means you cause the angle of attack at the tip of the wing to be less than it is at the root. So the root of the wing will reach its critical stalling angle before the tip. This is called wash-out, and is used by many designers to produce gentle stall characteristics. The ailerons, along the trailing edges at the outer portions of the wing, remain effective at very low speeds because, with wash-out, these portions of the wing continue to give lift at low speeds after the inner sections have stalled – the aircraft descends rapidly, but still under control.

Wash-out, however, has the great disadvantage that at high speeds (negative angles of incidence at the tip) the airstream bends the wing-tips downwards and thus imposes very high loads on the wing structure. Also in inverted flight, the wash-out becomes 'wash-in', and at high speeds a position can be reached when the inner part of the wing is being forced by the airflow 'downwards' (towards the earth), and the entire weight of the aircraft plus this additional load has to be taken by the wing-tips. There are other aerodynamic means by which nearly the same beneficial effects can be achieved, which are preferable to 'wash-out', but more difficult to design. Good flying qualities at low speeds are particularly desirable on a glider, which, unlike an aeroplane, is for much of the time flying at speeds near the stall.

Airbrakes. Imagine coasting a car downhill at 40 m.p.h. without brakes and having to judge accurately the point at which it will come to rest after reaching the bottom. A similar problem faces a glider pilot during his landing approach, complicated by the fact that the varying strength and direction of the wind will affect his angle of glide.

Airbrakes are nowadays fitted to all high-performance sailplanes, to simplify this problem. When opened, they destroy the lift over the section of each wing behind them, and so steepen the angle of glide. By putting them on and off during his approach, the pilot can control his glide in rather the same way as the pilot of an aeroplane, who can stretch his glide to any extent by a burst of power from his engine. The airbrake control is usually a lever in the same position, and operating in the same sense, as the engine throttle lever of an aeroplane. 'Brakes on' has the same effect as 'engines off', and vice versa. But unlike the aeroplane, the glider cannot in an emergency 'go round again' – the pilot must get it right first time.

Airbrakes have an additional advantage of the utmost importance. When applied at high speed, they add greatly to the drag of the aircraft, and so limit the maximum speed which it can reach in a vertical dive (terminal velocity, or T.V.) to one within the safety limits of the structure.

In the very rough air sometimes found inside storm-clouds, it is possible, when flying blind, to lose control of the aircraft, and prior to the days of airbrakes, sailplanes have been known to break up by exceeding their safe maximum speeds in dives out of control. The pilot of a modern sail-plane, if he finds his speed building up towards the danger point, has merely to clap on his airbrakes, and this ensures that he cannot pass it.

If everyone is still there, let us now apply the above to the design of a training glider. The top plate facing p. 64, shows a Primary, the cheapest and lightest flying device possible. The wings are of rectangular plan. Flying characteristics are vice-less in the extreme, because the machine is so light, and because, as it cannot fly fast (and certainly should not fly upside-down), a generous degree of wash-out can be put into the wing.

Numerous lengths of piano wire or cable prevent the wings from folding upwards in flight or downwards on the ground, though a very heavy landing has been known to break the landing wires, whereupon the wing-tips sag to the ground in a dispirited manner. The Primary flies at around 22 to 25 m.p.h. Its minimum sinking speed is poor, its maximum gliding angle steep, its penetration atrocious. The pilot is rather wind-swept but much, much safer than he looks. The reader may or may not be glad to learn that the Primary is now obsolete, and hardly ever used in gliding clubs. Pictures of it are still, however, treasured by small newspapers in distant corners of the globe, and trotted out

A bunjie-launch for a primary glider at Dunstable.

The author with his Scud II.

The author and crew corkscrew their way through the Spanish Sierras with
a Sky sailplane's trailer on tow.

for reproduction beside any news paragraph reporting a fresh world gliding record of some sort or other, such as a climb to 40,000 feet or so, with the caption underneath (accurate, so far as it goes) – 'A Glider'.

Glider training is now, however, undergoing a peaceful revolution on to two-seater trainers, and sufficient statistical evidence has now been acquired to show that, *with properly trained instructors*, such training is more efficient, safer, and so cheaper than the older method.

On these types of aircraft the trainee is brought up to the 'C' certificate standard. British requirements for the A, B and C certificates are as follows:

'A' – a straight glide of 30 seconds' duration.
'B' – two glides of 45 seconds followed by a flight of one minute including an S turn, or by one right-hand and one left-hand circuit each of one minute's duration.
'C' – a soaring flight of 5 minutes carried out above the altitude of launch.

The newly fledged pilot now progresses to an Intermediate sailplane. As regards the terms 'glider' and 'sailplane', the latter is a name for the more efficient glider, which is used for soaring – *i.e.* flights in which height is gained by using upcurrents after the launch. A Primary is a glider, but not a sailplane. A 'Sky' is both.

A sailplane is clearly much more refined aerodynamically, than is an elementary glider. Cantilever and tapered wings of high aspect-ratio and a well streamlined fuselage give much better penetration, and the reduced drag also enables minimum sinking speeds to be somewhat lowered. To the simple instruments fitted in the training aircraft may be added blind-flying equipment, and the addition of a parachute, and air-brakes, makes possible the first experiments in learning the art of blind flying. In such aircraft the learner trains further in the art of advanced soaring, and eventually achieves his 'Silver C'. This is an International Badge, for which the tests, as mentioned in Chapter 1, are: a flight of minimum duration 5 hours; a flight of minimum distance 50 kilometres; and a flight with a minimum climb of 1,000 metres. Having reached this stage, he is in the lower ranks of the élite, and could probably tell most aeroplane pilots one or two things they don't know, though it is unlikely that he would try.

With an intermediate sailplane of say 15 metres' span it is possible to achieve the next stage, the 'Gold C', but this of course is easier in a still more advanced sailplane such as the Sky, of 18 metres' span.

The requirement for the International Gold C are: a duration flight of 5 hours (if the pilot has already a Silver C his duration flight for this badge will suffice); a distance flight of 300 kilometres and a gain of height of 3,000 metres (approximately 10,000 feet).

Finally come the three Diamonds. A pilot adds a Diamond to his Gold C for each of the following achievements: a flight to a goal declared before take-off of at least 300 kilometres; a climb of 5,000 metres (about 16,500 feet); and a distance flight of 500 kilometres.

This last test is obviously extremely difficult in our restricted island. But any or all of these tests are much easier of achievement in hot countries, so that it is inaccurate to equate the mere number of International Badges in one country as against another as a measure of the relative skill of their pilots.

The observant reader may have noticed from the above that, after passing his 'C' Certificate tests, the average glider pilot today is to a considerable degree on his own, and has to learn the subsequent steps by solo practice and by what he can pick up from lectures or the talk of others. An obvious gap exists for a high-performance two-seater sailplane in which his training can be carried on, to enable him to progress more rapidly to the top levels.

Although such machines were built in Germany before the war, and many new post-war designs are in advanced stages there and elsewhere, in England we have not, at the time of writing, got anything of the sort actually in the air. The British Gliding Association sponsored a high-performance two-seater design contest in 1946, and seven years later the winning design is in process of construction. In my view, the present supremacy of British gliding, so laboriously achieved after more than 15 years' effort in 1952, will prove only temporary unless we can get such a machine in quantity use very shortly.

The motive power of a glider is, of course, gravity, the same power which gives its velocity to a falling stone.

To retain height in level flight, energy is extracted from the energy in the rising air in which the glider is flying, and it is a simple matter to calculate how much is involved.

One horsepower equals 33,000 ft./lb. per minute of work, or 550 ft./lb./sec. An advanced single-seat sailplane weighs, all up, say 825 lb. At its optimum flying speed in still air it loses height at the rate of 2 feet per second. The power required to lift it up again this 2 feet in one second=

$$\frac{825 \times 2}{550} = 3 \text{ h.p.}$$

In a cumulo-nimbus cloud, rates of climb of the order of 40 ft./sec. are not unusual. The power required to lift the sailplane at this speed is $3 + \dfrac{825 \times 40}{550} = 63$ h.p.

When one considers how a sailplane, from a wing area of say 200 sq. ft., extracts power of this order from the small area of the atmosphere which it occupies, some idea of the vast powers concealed in a single convection-cloud can be obtained. The energy generated by an atomic explosion compares unfavourably with the power generated by a meteorological phenomenon of small order. It is fascinating to consider that the ingenuity of the designer and the skill of the pilot makes it possible to tackle engines of such blind incredible power in a craft constructed of a few square feet of plywood and fabric.

5

ON BATHWATER

The world is divided, broadly speaking, into two types of minds: those which wonder why the bathwater always spins out of the plug the same way round (indeed, why does it spin at all?) and those which don't. At school they were called respectively Moderns and Classics.

The sport of sailplaning, however, attracts all sorts, so let me say that, even if you are a Classic, it is worth studying this problem a little closer.

Before we go any further, a word of warning. Many of the keenest enquirers have been nearly driven to drink on observing the bathwater apparently going out the wrong way round after all. (The right way is anti-clockwise in the Northern hemisphere, clockwise in Australia.) This may be due to one of the following causes:

(*a*) Often, I am told, it may be an optical illusion, which can be destroyed by dropping, say, a spot of lather on the swirling surface of the funnel, which spot can then be followed round by the eye.

(*b*) You started off with the water in initial motion the wrong way.

(*c*) The bath isn't big enough and introduces undesirable local topographic features. This can easily be cured by buying another one of at least twice the size. To be quite sure of results the bath should be some hundreds of miles across with the plug in the centre.

(*d*) The earth has stopped rotating.

In the subsequent endeavours to explain this complex matter I may seem to dodge about at times in rather a kaleidoscopic way, but be patient. True indeed is the old saying that bathwater runs deep.

The reader may be under the delusion that if he caused a frictionless body to be launched in any direction at, say 80 m.p.h., it would (*a*) pass out of his sight in a straight line and, if he waited long enough, it would (*b*) eventually re-appear on the opposite horizon and hit him on the back of the head. Nothing could be further from the truth. Even (*a*) is only logical if you are a Flat-Earther, and one may as well tell our Flat-Earth readers at once to skip the rest of this chapter.

To put my remaining reader in his place, I will now give a diagram of what actually *would* happen in the above circumstances:

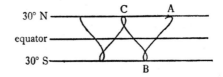

10 *Path of a body projected due E on a rotating sphere at a velocity of* 80 *m.p.h.*

Let us now take a couple of oblate spheroids as follows:

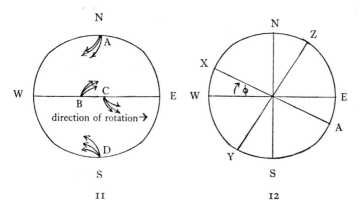

The globe rotates from west to east. If one stands on the Equator one is moving from west to east at around 1,000 m.p.h. If one stands at the Pole one is not. This is why penguins look so placid.

If Figure 11 is a model of this, duly rotating, and one were to pour a dollop of treacle on to the North Pole (point *A*), it would, as it flowed down, be continually encountering a surface moving with increasing velocity: in fact, it would tend to get left behind all the time, and would follow the path shown, curving to its *right*.

The same thing would happen, the other way round, if the treacle were to move upwards from the Equator (point *B*). Here it will flow on to continually slower-moving territory, so will tend to catch up, i.e. it will also turn *right*.

A glance at the flows *C* and *D* on the same diagram will show at once that, for the same reasons, in the Southern hemisphere the treacle will turn *left*.

So much for objects moving north or south. Pretty simple, but the next bit is much stickier.

In Figure 11, one can say that the globe is rotating round *NS* with an angular velocity of 360° in 24 hours, and round *EW* with an angular velocity of zero. It is because of this nil velocity that a dollop of treacle flowing round the Equator would not be deflected in any direction. You might think that a dollop flowing east–west in *any* latitude would not be deflected, but you would be instantly degraded back to Form IV if you said so.

Figure 12. If you are misguided enough to live at *X*, your rotation round *NS* could be equally accurately represented as a simultaneous rotation (at different speeds) round *XA* and *YZ*, at right angles to *XA*.★ If you can't understand this it's too bad, but you will not be lonely. It is a 'resolution of angular motion', and anyone who has navigated in a cross-wind or cross-current, using a triangle of velocities, will see a parallel.

Poor *X* may therefore imagine himself as existing on two superimposed globes, one rotating on an axis *XA* and the other on an axis *YZ*. If, having realised this, he is still bold enough to move in any direction, as far as Globe 1 (rotating about *YZ*) is concerned, he is on the Equator, and won't be deflected in any direction if he moves along it. As far as Globe 2 is concerned, however (rotating about *XA*), he is on the North Pole and in the position of our dollop of treacle starting from *N* in Figure 11, and he will be tactfully edged round to the right as he breaks into a trot.

As I am writing this in bed with a dose of 'flu and a tem-

★ This is where $\sin\phi$ (pronounced 'sign fie') creeps in to tell us exactly *what* speeds, but, shuddering from head to toe, we crush the loathsome thing under our strongly shod foot and hurry on.

perature of 102°, I can thoroughly sympathise if this is the last straw. A wiser (and cooler) writer than I would have funked it and slipped by with the magic words 'It can be shown that . . .'

Put Figures 11 and 12 together and we get FERREL'S LAW:

> *All bodies moving in the Northern hemisphere tend to deviate to the right; in the Southern hemisphere, to the left.*

Pause, whilst we take a couple of oblate spheroids.

To return to the bathroom. Elevate the plug, and you create an area of low pressure (*L*, Figure 13). It must have puzzled you before (unless you are already a Ferrelite) that, when such areas appear on the weather map, the air doesn't simply rush in from all sides and fill them up.

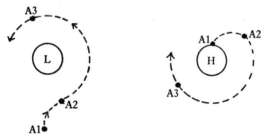

13   *Rotation of winds round low- and high-pressure areas in the northern hemisphere*

Let us take a particle at A_1. It starts to rush, but immediately it starts to move Ferrel steps in and starts turning it right (in the Northern hemisphere) as at A_2. Now it is subject to two forces. If the attraction of *L* momentarily increases, so does *A*'s velocity, Ferrel increases, and *A* swings out again. If Ferrel pulls *A* further away from *L*, pressure at

L decreases still further. So equilibrium is reached with A moving in a circle round L, along the isobars instead of, as one would expect, at right angles to them.

Now make L an H. A_1 starts to move out from the high-pressure area, is swung right to A_2, and so on. In each case the high- or low-pressure area becomes encased in revolving winds, and look as if they might well persist indefinitely. But, at ground-level, the wind-speed will be retarded by ground friction, so here Ferrel will weaken and the *surface* wind will blow obliquely into a low-pressure centre. Thus there is in fact a leak, at ground-level, into or out of these otherwise watertight systems.

This is the reason for the veer of wind with height which is a common problem of the sailplane pilot. It will be seen that this veer will be greater on high-wind days than low-wind ones, as ground friction will then be greater.

And so we come to a common question of sailplane pilots: Do thermals rotate? On the face of it, Ferrel is too small and slight to cause the rotation of so small a system as a thermal. But one has constantly seen dust devils, and pictures of waterspouts, all rotating madly, and the inference is very attractive that at least some thermals do the same. This would then endow a thermal, once started, with a sort of vacuum-cleaning power, whereby new air could only be sucked into the thermal along the ground-levels, where it is hottest, and so answer one of the difficulties of most theories: How does a thermal manage to go on for so long, once it has started?

The idea once mooted, that the hot air had a sort of capillary attraction which allowed millions of small bubbles to form and stick to, say, grass-stems, which were all released when the system became overcharged, has long been abandoned. It seems much more believable that, once an upcurrent starts, it actually sucks in new supplies of air from all sides at ground-level, and thus is supplied, as it browses along, with large quantities of fresh warm air, whilst at higher levels the intake of cold air is restricted by auto-rotation.

Anyway, it is comforting to think that Ferrel sets quite a problem to the master button-pusher of the next war. After gazing gloomily at Figure 10, which way does he have to point a rocket which he is going to set off from, say, M——, and which he firmly intends to land in N—Y—, after travelling at about three times the speed of rotation of the globe?

(Since this was written, far more complicated and in-comprehensible theories to account for thermal formation and persistence have been formulated. Wondrous adjectives such as 'termatectonic' and 'barostromatic' are bandied to and fro across professorial tables, whilst high brows glisten in the lamplight. But not here, oh Lord, not here!)

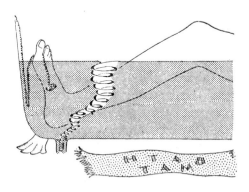

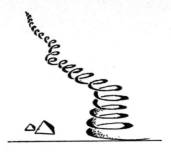

Multiply the bath-plug vortex by anything up to 10,000, and you have a picture of a waterspout or dust devil. This again illustrates the odd tendency of water or air to spin when provoked by an area of low pressure.

The following was written by R. H. Swinn, Chief Instructor of the Egyptian Gliding School.

The dust devils used by our School generally start their life in a tented camp about 500 yards away from our line of launch; this area lies outside the airfield. Their frequency may be anything from five minutes to every half-hour, and in most cases they are followed closely by a little brother dust devil, which is a modest little chap and trails along about 100 to 150 yards behind. When the cycle of frequency of the dust devil's birth is interrupted, as for example when a local change of wind takes place – as often occurs in mid-afternoon, when the wind can be seen blowing the chimney smoke in four different directions over an area of two miles square – energy is released to give birth to several tremendous dust devils and our tented camp is pleased to show us that it can produce the largest in the area. On these occasions

78

the dust devil often reaches 500 yards in diameter, a majestic swirling mass of sand moving at a leisurely pace along the edge of the aerodrome; its slow pace tends to belie its tremendous power, but a stroll through its outer wall and on into its milling vortex robs one of his breath, and has long ago taught me to think of them with the greatest respect.

The technique we use for flying in these dust devils is to keep a sharp eye on the tented camp whilst one is making normal training flights, and when a dust devil is seen to start, wait a few seconds for it to develop and gather a good body of sand, noting well its direction of rotation and line of travel. (The direction of travel in its early stages near the ground is not always directly downwind but in a line that deviates to the side on which the dust devil rotates in the downwind direction.)

The glider is launched and the release made at around 500 feet; the pilot turns towards the dust devil and cuts his speed as he approaches it to the minimum consistent with the control of the glider. As he nears the whirling column of sand he makes a circle on the outside of the dust devil against the direction of rotation, care being taken to give it a wider berth on the downwind side. In the light of the variometer reading on this initial circle, closer contact is made with the column or a hasty retreat is beat to a safer orbit.

Of the large number of flights I have made in these dust devils I will describe one which combines most of the features I have met with in the others.

On the day of this flight I was doing dual instruction, with the French high-performance machine (Air 100) lying at the launching point. A dust devil had built up in the tented camp. I landed the T-21B and dived into the Air 100. After being launched to 500 feet, I released and travelled rapidly in the direction of the rising column of sand. Unfortunately I had forgotten to note the direction of rotation, and near it its direction could not be clearly seen. I stayed away from the swirling mass, watching its root for evidence of rotation, until I saw a large mass of sand being flung round anticlockwise.

Accordingly I now made my approach in a clockwise direction, describing a fairly large circle, during which my variometer was giving its maximum reading. A too tight turn on the downwind side put a part of my inside wing into the vortex; the shock threw me into the straps and the wing bent in an alarming manner. This central area of greatly reduced pressure is something to be experienced to be believed. Closely following on this was the shock of hitting the area of greatest uplift just outside the central core. The net result was that the machine was thrown completely out of the column.

Whilst flying just outside the column and licking my wounds prior to getting to grips with it again, I noticed that the base was travelling in a line that would bring it directly over a large store of coal that is used to fire the Egyptian State Railway engines. Avoiding flying in the influence of the dust devil, I flew around it and waited for the base to strike the coal yard. Suddenly black masses of coal dust were being flung violently into the column and climbing at an alarming rate. I turned into the dust devil and was quickly engulfed in this black mass.

I thought to look down the centre of the vortex to see if it was as clear as had been those of my experience in the past. Tightening my turns, I whirled nearer and nearer to its centre, being pressed firmly down in my seat until I thought I would go through it. The machine, I felt, must be standing on its wing tip, and then suddenly I was looking down the vortex of the dust devil with the coal dust forming a dense wall, the whole of which gave one the impression of looking down a gigantic chimney. Needless to say, the view was obtained in snatches, as I was being thrown about violently, on one occasion passing through the centre of the vortex with a terrific downward plunge, only to be arrested with a violent shock and flung upwards again on my spiralling path. Looking at my altimeter for the first time, I found it had passed the 4,000 feet mark and was going round like the second hand of a clock.

Into the edge of the vortex I went again, thrilled with the thought of seeing 4,000 feet of swirling coal dust form a huge chimney from me to the ground. But I was to be disappointed, as now the chimney hung in the air with its base swirling many hundreds of feet above the ground, and it was beginning to bend half-way up so that only a restricted view of the interior of the funnel was available. For a moment I had that horrible feeling one gets when looking over the edge of a high building.

With bits of paper and much coal dust whirling round me, I settled down to keep in the outer wall of the funnel until its bottom end reached me, to get an impression of what happened when this arrived and the base passed me on its upward journey. I have no recollection at what height this happened, but I recall clearly the odd surges of lift and zero replacing the racing stream of the dust devil, followed by a normal rate of sink whilst, like a huge tortured snake, the gyrating mass swung upwards over my head, its exposed end looking like a huge frayed garden hose.

I kept my circles fairly tight for some time after passing the base of the funnel, and retained my position to feel the after-effects which trail along in the funnel's path; but on this occasion everything became as smooth as a mill-pond. Checking my bearing and height, I found I was 7,200 feet high and over the town of Maadi. I returned to the Heliopolis Aerodrome and continued with dual instruction.

Dust devils have no regular habits and vary in size from a foot in diameter (in which case they absolutely race along the ground) to many hundreds of yards across.

The conditions which appear to be necessary for the birth of a dust devil are intense heating of the air just above the ground in a wind-shadow, such as the leeward side of a hangar, or many small wind-shadows such as the tented camp mentioned. The latter seems to be the most efficient, as the constant feeding in of small bodies of superheated air over a large distance builds the dust devil into a thing of blind fury.

In speaking of intense heating, one must remember that one cannot put one's bare hand on the sandy surface during the day, and concrete, etc., is worse still, whilst to touch accidentally a metal surface gives rise to language that is in itself sufficient to start a thermal.

Outside our hangar there is a large stretch of wind-sheltered concrete which becomes intensely hot. In this area, close to the foot of the hangar, one can start up one's own little devils on occasions by a quick sweep of a signalling bat* from shoulder level in circular and downwards direction to a point almost touching the ground; one must step rapidly back or the vortex that is set up is spoilt. Such a miniature thermal starts about a foot in diameter and quickly assumes a conical shape about two feet high, moving along the ground at a walking pace. Its rotation increases very rapidly,

* A signalling bat is the shape of a large ping-pong racket.

until one has the impression of a whirling snake in front of one. As it reaches the edge of the concrete a little sand is thrown up and the thermal dies away. One wonders what initial energy is required to keep the thermal going.

Regarding the direction of rotation, this varies from thermal to thermal. I have been able to observe that the direction of rotation is decided at the beginning of the life of the dust devil when it is just breaking away from the ground. For example, if the left side of the thermal (facing down-wind) strikes an obstruction as it begins to break away, the direction of rotation is then anti-clockwise. In the event of the obstruction being on the right, it will be clockwise.

I have carried out a few experiments in changing the direc-tion of rotation of the smaller dust devils. The most success-ful of these was to drive a truck at the dust devil at a fairly high speed, passing through the side of the dust devil rotat-ing towards the oncoming truck. In one case only was the direction of the dust devil's rotation changed; in this case it was broken at its base completely, and it struck again some 200 yards further on, rotating in the opposite direction. (Since writing these notes I have seen the direction of rota-tion of a dust devil of a diameter of 5 yards changed com-pletely by merely passing over a small trench with the exca-vated mound of sand lying along its edge, the whole lying at an angle of 45 degrees to the line of travel of the dust devil.)

A dust devil when working well over the desert will, on striking houses, collapse completely near the ground, but continue to rotate above the houses, the bottom of the fun-nel ascending slowly. If the area to be traversed is not too great, the funnel will strike again behind the houses, but if the area of the houses is of considerable extent the funnel will not strike again and will recede upwards.

Passing over a hill of gentle slopes and of a height of 100 feet, the funnel will show a great burst of energy as it strikes the foot of the hill and then a quick weakening of power as it climbs the slope with only the downwind edge of the dust devil sweeping the ground with sufficient force to raise dust. At the very top of the hill all ground action ceases; then just over the top rotation can be detected again, whilst at the foot of the hill on the leeward side very violent rotation builds up, and at this stage the rotation is more violent than in the funnel's original state prior to its striking the hill.

The action of the dust devil as it passes over a depression in the ground is very interesting and varies according to the nature and size of the depression. In the case of a sand pit of a depth of 70 feet, the vortex did not reach the bottom, but a widening of the funnel took place and the base of this mass lessened its speed of rotation, sweeping about six feet above the floor of the pit with occasional little isolated whirlpools reaching out of the main mass to strike the floor of the pit. A pit with steep sides breaks up the bottom of the funnel.

A pit 30 feet deep with smooth, gradually sloping sides fed the funnel to a hissing, madly whirling mass that threw up great masses of sand. The funnel hung back in the pit and a great bend took place in the main mass which was carried by the free air above the pit. In this case the root of the funnel finally left the pit to align itself some distance further on under the main mass; but in one case the main column broke away and left the base of the funnel rotating in the pit to die out in a few seconds, the funnel of the main mass striking again a little distance outside the pit.

There seems to be a very close relation between the strength and life of a dust devil and the amount of visible suspended matter it contains – so much so that I strongly suspect that the absorption of the sun's rays by this swirling mass adds new energy to the funnel and makes it almost independent of ground-collected hot air for its continued life. I have not yet been privileged to see the spectacle of a dust devil extending from the ground into cloud. But I have, flying the T-21B solo, once entered a dust devil at 400 feet and stayed with it into cloud; but in the base of the cloud only the odd bit of paper could be detected being carried along.

I have been given a pair of sun glasses of polarised material having a reddish tint; a glance through these glasses transforms a bright blue sky into a glider pilot's paradise; columns of rising air having a slight dust content are seen everywhere. I have learned, however, from experience that not all the columns seen can be used, as many having the appearance of being relatively near are in fact lying a good distance back from their apparent neighbour.

A snag is that as one gets within a distance of around 500 yards of the dust column, the spectacles do not function any more, which calls for a technique of lining up one's glider with the thermal when still a good distance away. This technique is not as easy as it would appear, but it is sufficiently successful to have opened up quite new fields of soaring on most days.

Soaring one day on the Ataka mountain range near Suez, I saw approaching the mountainside a rather large dust devil with its column of whirling sand very well defined and rising to a considerable height. I put myself into a position to fly into it with a view to seeing what effect the mountain barrier would have on it. I flew into the funnel when it was about 200 yards from the face of the mountain. For a moment after entering the funnel all was well; then suddenly I was flung up in the most alarming manner, and by the time

I realised my position I was well over 1,000 feet above the mountain top. Things had happened so quickly and with such violence that I was unable to form any clear recollection of the effect of the dust devil striking the mountainside; by now the funnel was clearly outlined a little distance back from the top of the mountain, but the base of it was hanging in the air at a little less height than I was at. Flying straight for it, I was surprised to find that although the distance was apparently short I was well below the base of the funnel when I reached it, and I found no lift. Beating a hasty retreat to the mountain top again, I found the usual 'down' behind the crest and I had to make a most undignified return to the landing ground on the other side *via* a very rocky gully, much to the delight of my students whom I had previously instructed never to approach this gully under any circumstances.

6

A GLANCE (RATHER NERVOUS)
AT THE WEATHER

It is not my purpose in this book to attempt an exposition of the science of meteorology. It is a subject for experts, and clearly I am unqualified. If I were to attempt a description of such matters as the mathematics of wave-formation or the ingenious device of the tephigram, I might blow the gaff on how little I know; and on this one point I try hard to keep an absolutely unclouded mind. A bibliography will be found on page 218, to which interested readers are referred.

No one can join a gliding club without automatically absorbing a great deal of weather knowledge in the most painless way. On the subject of the air, however, there is one point on which I do feel absolutely clear, and that is that almost anything *can* happen, and occasionally does. Meteorology gives us a set of general rules which apply most of the time, particularly in dealing with large masses of air. But freak local conditions do continue to give both pilots and meteorologists the surprises of their lives.

For many years an odd experience, related by a sailplane pilot to a meteorological friend, would bring incredulity or disbelief. Now, however, a fruitful basis of mutual respect has been built up in this country largely by the work and personality of men like Sir David Brunt, Dr R. S. Scorer and F. H. Ludlam. And today there are few experiences which are not eagerly seized on by these meteorologists, who show the utmost ingenuity in framing suggested ways in which the phenomenon described might have occurred.

However, the explanation of why something *has* happened is, in the user's eyes, a minor subject compared with a reliable forecast of what is likely to be going to happen, and in Great Britain we live in a country where weather forecasting could hardly be more difficult. But the more that is learnt about the behaviour of the air, the more accurate can be our forecast of what it is likely to do tomorrow.

The characteristics of any mass of air depend very largely on where the air has come from, so the first thing to do is to trace it back to its origin.

There are certain broad regions of the globe where most of the character-formation of the air takes place. So far as we are concerned in this country, where most of our weather comes to us from the west, the two perhaps most important are the arctic regions around Iceland and Greenland, and the warm moist regions to the south, in the Atlantic ocean.

Arctic air is, of course, cold, and being cold it cannot hold much moisture: therefore it is dry and clear. When it moves our way and reaches our coasts, the sun's rays easily penetrate it and so are able to heat the surface of the earth. The warmed ground heats up the surface layer of the cold air, and so we get good convective, thermal conditions, with cumulus clouds, visibility to the horizon, and showers of rain or hail; an example being a typical cold, clear, showery spring day – daffodil weather, and good weather for the sailplane pilot.

Air coming to us from the sub-tropical regions of the Atlantic far to the south-west is the very reverse of this.

Being warm, it carries a lot of water-vapour which it has absorbed from the surface of the sea, and is hazy. Thus when it reaches our coasts the sun's heat cannot so easily reach the ground, and thermals do not form so readily. This is the moist and muggy weather of summer, or the endless grey south-westerly drizzle of winter.

The main large-scale weather situation that interests us is that which arises when two such fundamentally different streams of air meet each other, the titanic area of conflict thus formed being called a front.

The important point to remember here is that the cold air is denser than the warm. What happens at the front therefore, depends on whether the cold air is moving faster than the warm, or the reverse: whether the knife is catching up on the butter, or the butter on the knife.

The first situation creates a *cold front*, the second a *warm front*.

In a cold front, cold, dry north-westerly air cuts in under warm, moist south-westerly air, and shovels it up at a fairly sharp angle, almost as a plough turns up the furrow.

The moist air is thus abruptly lifted, and forms a vast line of cumulo-nimbus cloud, which may stretch for hundreds of miles along the line of the front, producing heavy rain or hail. On the ground, the observer is at first in the south-west air-stream, and the sky clouds rapidly over. The clouds get darker, rain starts to fall, which rapidly increases to a downpour, with possibly short, sharp hail or thunderstorms. As the front arrives the wind blows gustily and within a few minutes the rain may stop, the sun come out, and the wind change abruptly to north-west, in a clear blue sky. Downwind the retreating line of huge clouds can be seen, from horizon to horizon, with the rain beneath it.

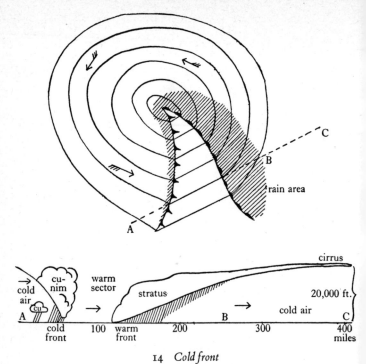

14   *Cold front*

A major cold front obviously produces titanic areas of lift, but is usually too big and wild to tackle. The sailplane pilot is usually quite satisfied to explore the secondary fronts, comparatively small rearguard actions in which the cold air is clearing up pockets of resistance after the main battle has passed over.

In a warm front, the south-westerly air-stream overtakes the polar air, and proceeds to try and suffocate it. It creeps up over it at a very small angle, creating an enormously extended shelf of featureless stratus cloud, which may extend for hundreds of miles ahead of the front itself.

The observer therefore, in a westerly wind, with clear skies, at first sees a very high haze creeping up overhead, possibly of cirrus clouds. Slowly this thickens and gets lower, eventually becoming a uniform sheet of stratus cloud covering the sky, whilst the wind backs towards the south. As the front approaches, this sheet gets slowly thicker, greyer and lower and it may start to drizzle, gradually turning to continuous rain. There is no dramatic moment of clearance, but

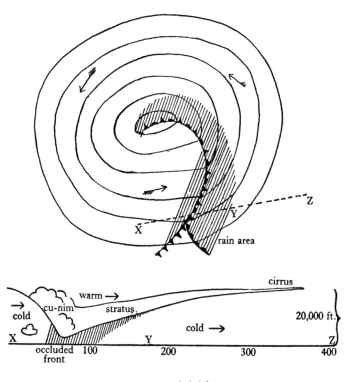

15   *Occluded front*

eventually the wind veers to south-west, the sky slowly clears, and warmer and moister weather prevails.

Although small-scale phenomena such as the bathroom vortex, a waterspout, or a dust devil may rotate either way, Ferrel sees to it that a large-scale system always rotates the same way. Hence, in the Northern hemisphere, depressions always rotate anti-clockwise, and anti-cyclones clockwise.

Thus the direction of the wind at any given spot does not necessarily indicate where the air-mass you are in actually originated, and one may get polar air blowing from the west or south-west, having come on a circular course from Icelandic regions.

When a polar air-stream meets a tropical air-stream to form a front or frontal system, what usually results is a depression: a circular mass of cold air rotating anti-clockwise which has trapped a wedge of warm air, like a rotating Dutch cheese with a slice cut out of it; the cheese being the cold air, the slice the warm air. The whole cheese, as it rotates, is moving across the face of the globe, in our part of the world usually from west to east.

The wedge of warm air is called the Warm Sector. At its front edge the warm air is creeping up over the cold, forming a warm front; at the rear edge the cold is undercutting the warm, creating a cold front. The cold front is travelling faster than the warm and closing up the gap, and when it has completely caught up and prised the warm air up from the ground entirely there remains a layer of cloud above. The resulting system is then called an occluded front.

When comparing the bluff, quick and powerful action of a cold front with the stealthy but irresistible tactics of the warm, one cannot help feeling that, of the two, the cold front is the more British arrangement.

Dream Lady (*dreamily, coming to life after a long silence*): But there is a lovely poem about a warm front:

> The South West wind doth endlessly blow
> And the small rain down doth rain;
> Oh Christ! That my love were in my arms
> And I in my bed again!

Me (*nervously*): Well, I'm not sure that you've got that exactly right. But it's certainly rotten weather for gliding.

7

THE SPIN TEST

Dream Lady (rising from her knees, where she has been ever since Chapter 1): I see you wear a parachute. Why?

Me: It is customary for sailplane pilots to wear parachutes for protection if they go into storm-clouds after big lift, although in modern machines with airbrakes I don't think there have been any cases of break-up owing to loss of control, such as used to happen in the early days. As a matter of fact, a bale-out in a big cumulo-nimbus isn't as simple as it sounds.

D.L.: Why not?

Me: There are several reasons. First, a glider parachute has to be able to open quickly at the low speeds at which a glider normally flies. But if, for instance, you got into a high-speed spiral dive (in an old machine without airbrakes) you might have to bale out at as high a speed as 200 m.p.h. The terminal velocity of a human body falling free is only 120 m.p.h.; therefore in such a bale-out, it is best to wait a bit whilst the wind-resistance *slows you down* before pulling the rip-cord, to avoid a tremendous jerk when the canopy opens. It always sounds to me a bit nerve-racking to cope with this when falling blind in cloud.

Then, one's speed of descent with a parachute is about 16 feet a second. But in a cumulo-nimbus you may easily be in air rising at twice this speed, so if you rip too soon you can easily go on going up. Of course, you won't know this

because you will still be falling through the air at 16 ft./sec.
But a German pilot was once kept bobbing up and down on
his parachute inside a cloud for over an hour, and got very
badly frost-bitten. So the rule is, if one has to bale-out in
cloud, to delay pulling the rip-cord until you fall out of the
base. But don't get het up about this, because it doesn't
happen – at least, I have never met anyone to whom it has.

D.L.: So you haven't ever had to use your parachute?

Me: No, and I don't expect I ever will (touch wood).

D.L.: Then doesn't it seem rather a waste of money and
weight?

Me: Er – no. As a matter of fact, my parachute *did* once save
my life.

D.L.: But I thought you said you had never used it?

Me: Neither I have.

D.L.: Explain yourself.

Me: Well, it wasn't only the parachute. It was also because I
was best man to a friend of mine in 1930, who gave me a
silver cigarette-case for my labours, although I must say it
was a sinecure to some of the best men I had been.

D.L.: I shall definitely resign my post unless you stop
maundering about like this and tell me what happened.

Me: Sorry. But you have to be so careful nowadays. Before
the war, I could tell the story with the feeling that it was
quite an adventure. But in these days, when the bank-clerk
sitting next to you in the railway-carriage turns out to have
been a paratroop at Arnhem, the whole thing was, in comparison, a cosy weekend country party. Anyway, it's quite
instructive, and you asked for it.

In 1937 the Germans held the first International Gliding
Championships ever organised. The venue was their

famous soaring centre on the Wasserkuppe, in the Rhön mountains.

We decided to enter a team and, as it happened, Slingsby was at the time building at his works a new high-performance sailplane, designed by Mungo Buxton, who had also designed my Hjordis. The Slingsby firm very sportingly decided to take the risk and complete three of these aircraft for us to take to Germany.

I say 'risk' because, in the normal way, a new design is usually built as a single prototype, which is then exhaustively tested and modified until one is quite sure she is right; and not until then does quantity production start. There was no time for this in this case, but Hjordis, designed and built by the same people, had proved immediately successful, so everyone, including myself, had considerable confidence in the new type.

The first machine was finished in April, and I went north for her test flying, which took place from York aerodrome. She proved beautiful to look at and to handle, and everyone congratulated everyone else on her success. A month went by, and in Coronation week I again went north for her final trials, the last item of which was to be her test for spinning.

Even today, when the causes of spinning and the design requirements for successful recovery from a spin are fairly well known, every machine has to be taken to a great height and stalled and spun deliberately before the designer can be quite certain that it is satisfactory in this respect. But I had never heard of a glider spinning viciously: in fact my own Hjordis refused to spin at all; and the King Kite had behaved so beautifully on all her trials so far that any idea of trouble never entered my head.

I was strapped into the cockpit and the celluloid cover was

put on over my head. Three hundred feet of wire cable was strung from the tail-skid hook of the towing aeroplane to my own nose-hook, and we took off.

It was a clear blue day with not a ripple in the sky. At 4,500 feet I pulled the release, and the aeroplane put down its nose and dived away to the distant earth. I floated along for a minute or so in the blissful quiet which is one of the abiding joys of the sport. Then I eased the stick gently back, and she started to climb. Slowly the speed fell off until, as the needle came back to just under 40, she gave a little shudder, and the stick went dead. I kicked on full left rudder, the nose rolled over, the earth tilted majestically up from underneath until it was right ahead of me, then started to revolve.

After half a turn the speed came up rapidly, I put on opposite rudder and centralised the stick in the normal way, the earth slowed down and returned quietly to its normal place beneath me. Good! I glanced at the altimeter: still 4,000 feet up, plenty of height for one more spin, the other way.

I eased back the stick once more, she climbed, slowed, faltered. I kicked on full right rudder, she rolled over like a gannet on to the dive. I let her spin a little longer this time, all seemed well, then moved the controls again to bring her out.

Nothing happened: the earth ahead went on revolving like an immense gramophone record, objects on it growing perceptibly larger.

Quickly I put the controls back to spinning position, adjusted the wing-flaps, and tried again, firmly. Still the spin went on, my speed increasing unsteadily and the hum of the wind outside growing to a roar. There was nothing more to be done; the time, so often anticipated, had come to abandon ship and take my first taste of the delights or otherwise of parachuting.

There was so much to do that I did not feel in the least worried, only faintly ridiculous that such a thing should befall me, a respectable City business man, husband and father. There was some mistake; these experiences should confine themselves to our professional heroes. But my next movements had been practised so often in imagination that they took place almost without volition.

I reached above my head for the cord releasing the cockpit cover, pulled it, and pushed the cover upwards. The gale outside lanced in underneath as it lifted, caught it from my hand and whirled it away. The wind shrieked and tore at my clothes, caught my glasses and whipped them off. The nearing earth became a green, unfocused, whirling blur. I let go of the controls and my hands went to the catch fastening the safety straps, clicked it open, and gave a reassuring pat to the sheathed handle of the parachute rip-cord.

The machine, freed of all attempt at human control, lurched about as it span in a curious idiot way, a body without a mind. I drew up my knees, leant over the left-hand side of the cockpit, and dived head foremost over the edge.

And now a dreadful thing happened. As I went over the side, it seemed to swing round and up at me with a vicious jerk, struck me across my chest and flung me back helplessly into my seat. The spin went on.

A second time I gathered myself together and leaped over the side, and a second time I was caught and bounced childishly back: it was as if I was struggling to break through the bars of an invisible but invincible cage. The spin went on. The blurred earth seemed now very near: in fact it was scarcely two hundred and fifty yards ahead.

It is curious but true that at a last moment such as this one's body, partly exhausted by former struggles, can nevertheless gather together sufficient physical energy to make a final effort surpassing previous ones. A third time I flung myself, still more violently, over the side. This time I got well out, head-first and well forward – almost free – the whirling outline of wings and fuselage was all around me, filling the sky. There was the most appalling bang, a violent blow, and I found myself once more back in my seat, hands and feet instinctively on the controls. The world swung violently overhead, slowed, stopped spinning, stopped spinning, the machine was on its back, only centrifugal force was holding me in – but the controls were biting the air again, life had come back into them, life in them was life in me. I pulled back on the stick, she came staggering round on the second half of a loop, I steadied her, and looked down.

The aerodrome buildings were a bare three hundred feet beneath. The raging gale in the exposed cockpit sank to a friendly breeze, apologising for losing its temper. I put down the landing flaps, did a half turn and landed, not a hundred yards from the clubhouse. I looked out, and saw my wife running towards me over the turf. My recording barograph showed that I had spun down like Satan from Paradise, two-thirds of a mile in one minute.

After a while I levered myself to my feet and stepped gingerly over the edge of the cockpit. As I did so I felt a violent cramping pain in my chest. Clearly I had strained my heart: you can't go doing things like this without paying for it, I thought.

I was helped into the clubhouse and lay down, waiting for the reaction. Every time I moved my heart gave a vicious tweak. Ten minutes later I put my hand to my waistcoat pocket for a soothing cigarette and brought out my metal case bent in a line across its centre to the shape of a three-dimensioned 'L'.

My last jump had got my weight so far forward, had so materially altered the trim of the machine, that the hidden vice had been overcome. As the wings bit the air at high speed, the machine was swung round with such violence that we found the main wingbolts, great rods of steel holding the wings to the fuselage, all four bent. And the side of the cockpit came round and hit my chest with a blow sufficient to break every rib in my body. But instead it caught my cigarette case fair in the middle, the force was distributed over an area, and I escaped with a set of internal bruises that kept me awake for the next three weeks, a cigarette case that will never open again, and a parachute that never had been opened, but nevertheless had given me the incentive to jump.

In the outcome, I was able to describe my spin sufficiently well for the experts to diagnose too small a rudder. A larger one was fitted, the machine was tested again with many safeguards. Although subsequent events showed that this was not the full answer, we took the three King Kites to Germany with two other machines, and in the fortnight the British team did cross-country flights totalling over 1,100 miles.

I was told that I should have known that you must always bale out on the *inside* of a spin, and that if, in a right-hand spin, I had dived over the *right*-hand side, I would have fallen cleanly and instantly down the centre of the corkscrew and, once clear of the machine, released my parachute and watched the glider spin down to its wreckage.

As it happened it was fortunate I did not know this, one of the elementary rules of parachuting which no one troubles to tell you; for the machine was saved. Even the cockpit cover was picked up, but slightly damaged, a mile away. The only permanent loss was my spectacles, and perhaps a few days cut off my old age.

Dream Lady: Is that all? If you call *that* an adventure, you ought to have been with me in Fulham in 1944 when a V1 fell within fifty yards of me. I was wearing a miniature of my grandmother in a locket round my neck and——
Me: There you are! I told you so.

8

STABILITY AND CONTROL

The last chapter illustrates one of the more complex problems facing the aircraft designer. In addition to spin recovery, there are the problems associated with the whole field of stability and control.

Early motorists will remember how the steering wheels of the first cars had to be wrestled with when at speed on rough roads, whereas today almost all cars will hold the road almost 'hands off' at all speeds. Similar requirements face the aircraft designer, complicated by the fact that his machine operates in three dimensions, and cannot slow down quickly, or below a certain speed, if it starts to become unmanageable.

In a book of this kind it is only possible to describe the bare outlines of a subject as complicated as the stability of aircraft. There are two main headings: static and dynamic stability.

To illustrate static stability, although it has been used before, I know of no better diagram than Figure 16. Ball *A*,

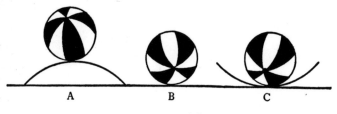

16 *Static stability*

balanced on an inverted cup, if pushed, will fall away from its initial position with ever-increasing velocity. It is *negatively* stable.

Ball *B*, on a flat, frictionless table, if pushed in any direction, will continue to move steadily in that direction until another force is applied to it. It is *neutrally* stable.

Ball *C*, in a cup, will, when moved, attempt all the time to return to its original position. It is *positively* stable.

But note that, in the case of ball *C*, it does not roll back to its original position and immediately stop there, but 'overshoots', and only comes to rest after a number of oscillations of decreasing size. This is where dynamic stability comes in.

An object (or system) is dynamically stable if the oscillations following a disturbance tend to die out. Strike a note on the piano, and the wire vibrates, but the vibrations gradually die out: the piano string is dynamically stable. If, once struck, the note were to continue at constant amplitude, this would indicate neutral dynamic stability; whereas if it were to increase it would be dynamically unstable. An example of dynamic instability familiar to some is the 'wheel-wobble' which sometimes occurs on aged cars.

Applying these concepts to a glider, in the pitching plane (nose up or down), imagine a glider descending at constant speed on a straight path, trimmed to fly 'hands off' ('stick-free'). The pilot pushes the stick forwards and depresses the nose, then lets go again.

A machine possessing negative static stability will then go on diving ever more steeply, gaining more and more speed until corrected by the pilot. If neutrally stable in pitch, it will continue to fly steadily, at an increased speed, in the new attitude in which it has been placed. If positively stable it will pull up its nose and tend to return to its original speed and flight path, but will be likely to overshoot and go into a slight climb. Now its dynamic stability characteristics will show themselves.

The wave-like path the glider will follow is called a 'phugoid', and Figure 17 shows the type of phugoid it will follow depending on its dynamic stability.

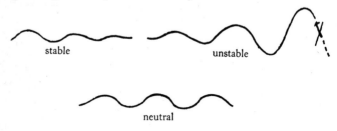

17   *Dynamic stability*

Obviously, for easy and safe handling, the pilot needs a machine with positive static and dynamic stability characteristics, so that if he gets into difficulties in cloud or elsewhere, his aircraft will be on his side; and the subtle design problems of achieving this are being increasingly understood.

Stability in the other dimensions of yaw and roll introduces other considerations, but I have probably written enough to indicate the general scope of the subject.

All these problems are now controlled in most countries within the requirements of a Certificate of Airworthiness, and the pilot is protected providing he does not start gaily trying to 'improve' the flying qualities of his machine by altering the controls or flying surfaces in any way – which invalidates his C. of A.

All British aircraft carry a placard in the cockpit setting out maximum speeds, maximum and minimum pilot weights and ballast requirements. In addition the Certificate of Airworthiness distinguishes three separate categories of aircraft: non-aerobatic, normal aerobatic and unrestricted aerobatic.

The second class, into which most sporting sailplanes fall, is stressed for all normal aerobatics, such as spins and loops, but only the third class is capable of inverted aerobatics such as outside loops and slow rolls. For aerodynamic and weight reasons, the ordinary sporting sailplane cannot be designed to come into the 'unrestricted' class, without sacrificing performance to an unacceptable extent.

A glider with a British Certificate of Airworthiness, flown within its category and its placard limitations and properly maintained, is as strong and safe as the best powered aircraft. In fact, with no fire risk and a much slower landing speed, it is possible to say it is even safer.

9

GETTING UP AND STAYING UP

 It must be realised that upcurrents, except for hill-lift, are not very strong near the ground, so that the requirement of a launch is to give the glider an initial height of between 1,000 and 2,000 feet.

In the case of hill-lift, however, all that is necessary is to get the glider into the air a few feet above the crest of the hill, although in light winds, when there is some doubt as to whether the upcurrent will be strong enough to enable the pilot to soar, an initial height of a few hundred additional feet is a great help. However, the cheapest and simplest launching method from the hill-top is by catapult, or 'shock-cord', the only requirement being a thick rubber rope and a number of willing runners. This method is usually called a 'bunjie-launch', for obvious reasons.

A metal ring spliced in the centre of the rubber rope is placed on an open hook on the nose of the glider, one enthusiast lies on his stomach and hangs on to a loop at the tail end of the aircraft which is facing into wind and down the hill, and the two free ends of the bunjie are spread out ahead of the machine in a V. From two to four stalwarts take hold of each end, and on the shouted instructions of the pilot proceed to walk, and then run, down the hill, stretching the rope. At the right moment the pilot shouts to the tail-holder to let go, and is catapulted forwards, the ring falling off his open nose hook as he passes over the launchers (see top plate facing p. 64).

The pilot immediately turns his machine to fly along the ridge from which he has taken off, and proceeds to tack to and fro, climbing in the upcurrent.

This method involves a take-off point on the top of a hill, so is not generally applicable to other sites. For taking off from the foot of a hill, or from flat sites, a winch is generally used. In its simplest form, this consists of a steel drum holding up to 3,000 feet of stranded wire rope (of about 20 cwt. breaking strain) on the back wheel of a car, which is jacked up and the free wheel locked. The wire is pulled out downwind, and attached to the quick-release hook on the glider. For take-off, the wire is wound in on to the drum at the necessary speed, from 35 to 45 m.p.h. during the initial part of the take-off, and the glider climbs steeply until it is nearly overhead of the winch, when the pilot operates his release.

The wire drops (it preferably has a small parachute near the glider end to soften its fall) and has then to be retrieved and towed out again to the launching-point. Modern winches are considerably more complicated, but the principle is of course the same.

A height of about 1 in 3 can be achieved with a good launch in a light wind, *i.e.* 1,000 feet, with a 3,000-foot cable run.

On an aerodrome with a good long runway, an auto-tow is rather simpler than a winch-launch. In this method, a car is attached with 1,000 feet of wire (which can be piano-wire) to the glider, and drives at a suitable speed along the runway. In this

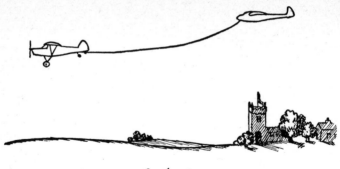

18 *Aero-tow*

case, the glider can achieve nearly the height of the length of wire itself.

The easiest, but unfortunately most expensive, launch is by aeroplane tow. Here a 300-foot cable is used, preferably of manilla rope or nylon, whose elasticity reduces the roughness encountered in a launch in gusty or unstable air. Owing to its lower stalling speed, the glider leaves the ground before the aeroplane, and the most usual procedure is then to fly sufficiently above the tailplane of the tug to ensure that the rope at the aeroplane tail-skid is pulling directly backwards so that the trim of the tug is not affected either way.

One of the great advantages of this method is that if, as the train flies along, an upcurrent is encountered, the aeroplane enters it first, and bobs up in front of the glider, which in turn bobs up as it enters the upcurrent itself a few seconds later. The glider pilot can thus actually see that he is in an upcurrent, and can be sure that he is in lift when he releases.

Except in certain cases of wave-lift, there is no need to climb above 1,500 or 2,000 feet for upcurrents: on good thermal days sailplanes have managed to 'get away' from as low as 250 feet although this calls for considerable skill;

and in the case of hill-lift, a good slope of 250–300 feet will give quite enough lift to sustain even Primaries in soaring flight. In fact, ridges of considerable altitude usually carry the disadvantage of being in cloud on many days when soaring would otherwise be possible.

The actual controls of a glider are identical with those of an aeroplane, with the important exception that, instead of a nasty vulgar throttle, the glider pilot has to use his wits to keep himself aloft.

When he finds a piece of air that is going up, the pilot naturally wishes to stay in it. If it is going up because it is surmounting a hill, he flies up and down along the crest of the hill. If it is thermal lift, it will probably take the form of air rising in a column or bubble, which drifts along with the wind. The sailplane is more likely than not to enter the thermal at an angle – i.e. one wing first, and this wing will accordingly lift and the sailplane will try and turn out of the rising air. It is important to realise that a glider will always try to turn out of lift, therefore the pilot immediately counters this, turns, say, 60° against the upflung wing, flies in this direction for a few seconds, watching his rate-of-climb indicator (variometer) and then commences a circle when this indicates steady lift.

A thermal column may be of small or large diameter, but small ones are usually low down, and the column naturally expands as it rises. Sometimes a thermal may be a mile or more across, but within the column some areas will be rising faster than others, and the pilot watches his variometer and tries to edge over to that side of his circle which is showing the best lift, either by flying in ovals or doing a figure eight. When circling, he flies all the time in true *air* circles, drifting

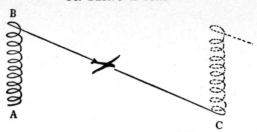

19 *Flight unit: cross-country flight*

with the wind. Since thermals are formed by the sun, they
are phenomena of the day, and die with the evening. All
distance flying therefore is in the nature of a race with time,
and the pilot who goes farthest is generally he who can get
the most rapid climb out of each thermal.

On any given day, each consecutive thermal is likely to
be of approximately the same strength as the previous one.
As the day goes on, thermal strength is likely to increase
gradually until about 5 p.m. (G.M.T.) and after this to
decrease gradually, although this is only a general rule, like
anything else to do with the air. Another likely similarity is
that the pilot will find the most active lift in each thermal in
a given layer of the air, and usually lift decreases below
1,500 feet. Therefore best climbs will be achieved by keeping within a given minimum and maximum altitude. If lift
falls off at, say, 4,000 feet much time may be wasted in screw-
ing a further 500 feet out of the thermal before setting off on
one's course.

The next point is to decide on the correct speed at which to
fly between one thermal and the next. This depends on the
average strength of the thermals on the particular day, and
the polar curve of the sailplane (p. 62).

Figure 19 shows one complete unit or cell of any cross-
country flight, consisting of a circling climb in a thermal

(AB) and the subsequent descending glide to the next piece of lift (BC). The pilot who will go farthest is he who can get from A to C quickest, and go on doing so all day. If the lift is strong it pays to fly fast from B to C, because although in doing so the machine will lose more height than another aircraft flying slowly, it will get to the next lift more quickly. It is a fairly simple matter to work out a cruising chart for any particular machine, based on its polar curve, and such charts, attached to the variometer, are being increasingly used by advanced pilots.

These charts are also useful to show the pilot the best speed at which to fly in downcurrents. If one visualises a thermal as somewhat the shape of a fountain, it will be evident that downcurrents are to be expected surrounding every thermal upcurrent, and this is almost invariably the case. When leaving the top of a thermal it therefore pays to put on extra speed in order to fly through the surrounding downcurrent quickly, and the cruising chart gives the correct speed for all conditions of vertical air motion.

But of course, if during a distance flight the pilot reaches a point where it seems possible that lift ahead may be scarce, he must either attempt to fly round the unfavourable area or else attempt to cross it at the speed giving him maximum range. This speed depends on the strength and direction of the wind in relation to his course. So in addition to maximum *speed* cruising charts, the pilot also needs a number of maximum *range* charts, and he switches from one to the other as need arises. The pilot who attempts to force the pace too much will find himself on the ground, compelled to watch his more cautious competitors sailing serenely overhead. It is a mortifying experience which comes to all sailplane pilots in time.

When reasonably high up, on cumulus days, the pilot can assess likely areas of lift by looking at the clouds ahead. If he leaves his thermal near the base of the cumulus capping it, and flies nearly downwind towards another cumulus, he is likely to enter the upcurrent creating it without much difficulty. But thermals have a limited life, and cumulus clouds form and dissolve like slow shellbursts, so that sometimes even this technique turns out to be an exasperating hunt after lift which vanishes just as you are expecting to reach it.

Underneath a cloud, the darkest area, indicating the greatest depth of cloud above, is usually the best for lift, and if one sees a dark line, with ragged edges, on the under-surface of any cloud, this may often indicate a large area of rising air.

As the sailplane gets lower, the pilot has to transfer his attention and his search for his next lift from the clouds above to the ground below. Now he looks for areas which are likely to be warmer than their surroundings. The roofs and streets of a town in sunlight are obvious sources of good lift, and dry, sandy or chalk soils give off more thermals than clay or other moist areas. An exceptionally good bet is the cooling tower of a power station, and on many days smoke and steam rising from these huge concrete cotton-reels can be seen as a wavering visible column right up to the cumulus cloud formed by this prodigious human waste of heat.

In 1946 the British national gliding competitions were held at an aerodrome near the big power station at Castle Bromwich, and on a day of no general lift, the competitors used to aero-tow to these cooling towers, and sail around overhead like a cloud of midges until they felt the urge for a cup of tea back at base.

When you want to find a warm spot for your deck-chair in the garden, you pitch it in the sun and out of the wind, in the lee of a wall or hedge. You could say you were sitting in a wind-shadow. The ground in the lee of the sheltering hedge gets warmer than its surroundings, and tends to create a thermal upcurrent, called a wind-shadow thermal.

In certain conditions, a band of lift can be found running parallel to a coast line, on a sunny day when a shallow sea breeze blowing onshore encounters a general wind blowing against it or at an angle to it. At the line of encounter, the opposing airs naturally create an upcurrent, and a sailplane can fly rapidly along parallel to the coast, sometimes a few miles inland, sometimes actually a few miles out to sea. The position of the upcurrent can frequently be determined by the line of cumulus clouds formed by it, which will be somewhat across the wind direction, and following the coast line.

On most cumulus days, however, these clouds tend to form in lines up and down wind, and sometimes these lines join up to form zebra-like stripes of cloud from horizon to horizon. These are the long-distance days, usually with a fairly fresh wind blowing. The rejoicing pilot can on such a day fly along under one edge of the 'cloud street' in practically a straight line, finding lift all the way, and on these days retrieving teams need full petrol tanks.

Cloud streets are sometimes formed when the whole air is rolling over like a series of gigantic contra-rotating drainpipes running up and down wind (see Figure 20). It will be seen that one edge of each line of cloud gives good lift and the other strong sink.

On such a day no sailplane pilot worthy of salvation would change places with any king in history. The air is clear and cold, like spring water, vibrant with life. The earth is a dapple of greens and browns, striped with the soundless racing shadows of the clouds. The sea is all shades of blue and amethyst, spotted with flecks of foam. And the pilot – he is free and proud and skilful as an eagle, the air is his and all the earth it bathes with its fresh and cleansing flood. His aircraft is part of him, his wings, sweeping silently in wide curves up to the clouds, darting in a swift straight glide to the next aerial fountain, dancing instinctively, almost without volition, as light and brilliant as the sunlit air.

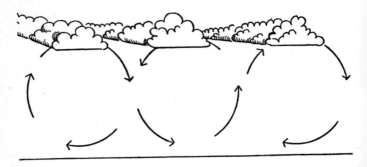

20　*Cloud streets : one of the upcurrent systems*

10

GOING WEST

The following flight, carried out in ideal cloud-street conditions, remains something of a classic, because its feasibility was worked out from observations over the three previous years, and it opened up a new and hitherto unsuspected direction for long-distance flying in Great Britain. Previously, flights downwind in north-westerly or westerly winds had seemed the only possibility for long distances, as only these winds, during the bulk of the year, provide suitable long-distance weather conditions; and this very much limited the range of anyone living in the London or Midland districts.

When this flight actually came off, in nearly every detail to plan, it won for me, besides the British distance record, the first British Gold C and the third in the International list. A day like this repays a hundredfold the scores of failures which make up the vast preponderance of one's attempts in this most elusive of all sports.

I have made dozens of equally ambitious plans in my time, and so has every other sailplane pilot worth his salt. But this is the rare story of the One That Didn't Get Away.

I remember the spring of 1938 as one of the golden seasons of the British gliding movement. Since July 1936 I had held the distance record, with a flight of 104 miles in Hjordis from Dunstable to Pakefield, on the Suffolk coast. This seemed nearly as far as one could go in a soaring, westerly wind from

Dunstable, so the next record involved breaking new ground.

Then on 17th April 1938, Kit Nicholson flew in his Rhönsperber 120 miles from Huish in Wiltshire, south-west to Bigbury-on-Sea. But he held the record for only one day, and on 18th April Sylvan Fox beat him with a 145-mile flight in his Rhönadler, in the same direction, from Huish to Fowey, in Cornwall.

That year, however, the spring unstable north-easters persisted in a way that they have not repeated since, right up to 30th April. What follows was written by me just after the flight on that day.

The newspapers always call it Buchan's third cold spell. Be that as it may, I have personally noticed that in each of the past four years we have had, between 20th March and 30th April, a spell of highly unstable north-east winds. In past years I have made plans to get a launch from the South Downs during this period – which have always come to nothing. But this year the advent of aero-towing at Heston, specially organised to be ready in time, made it easy, while the north-easterlies simultaneously obliged by blowing steadily for practically the whole period – to the confusion of farmers but the profit of sailplane pilots.

Going to the office on Friday 29th April, I looked wistfully up from the crowded city streets at the activity of a different sort going on overhead. It seemed too much to expect yet another such day to follow – but that evening the weather bureau said 'same again'. That meant a north-east wind, cloud streets forming as early as 9 a.m., with a tendency (in London, anyway) for the whole sky to cloud over later in the day. I asked whether this was not due to the influence of the North Sea. The weather people agreed that it was likely, and added that I would probably be safe from Salisbury onwards. It looked, therefore, as if part of the problem would be to get to Salisbury (65 miles) before, say, noon. This meant early breakfast, to be rigged and away from Heston by 10.30.

We spent a busy evening getting everything ready for an early start. I ruled out the line of flight on the map and studied the course as closely as possible. The conditions looked as though they might be very similar to my flight earlier in the month from Huish to Plympton, so I hoped I might find the same sea-breeze effect which I had then found so useful from Lyme Regis onwards. The course I mapped out, therefore, took me to Lyme Regis, thence out to sea and along the coast to Exmouth, then on towards Plymouth. As a matter of fact, on the actual flight I was seldom more than five miles off the course at any point.

On Saturday morning it didn't look very hopeful. The instability was there all right, but the wind was strong and far too northerly. We consequently left later than we had planned, said we'd be home to tea, and left behind luggage and money.

When we arrived at Heston, the sky looked marvellous. Tremendous streets ran up and down wind as far as the eye could see, and although the surface wind was almost due north, the upper wind, judged by the line of cloud streets, was north-east. This was confirmed by the met. people as 050° above 1,000 feet (I should have to make good a track of 250° to get round Sidmouth Bay). Across a 20 m.p.h. wind this was better than I had feared, but was quite bad enough. However, I hoped first for the favourable sea-breeze effect already mentioned, and second that the wind might drop with the combination of the approaching evening and conflicting sea breezes. I hoped for the latter from Bridport to Plymouth – which I formally declared as my goal. Now, as it happened, both these preconceived possibilities came true. Let us therefore be optimists always.

A last point was that with the big veer in the wind with height, it was clear that if I got into difficulties anywhere they would be increased by its northerly trend the lower I flew.

I make no apology for this long preliminary argument, because I am sure that previous planning of a long flight is of the utmost importance, particularly in England, where every really long flight must of necessity be in the nature of a goal flight.

As the result of delays and uncertainties, it was 11.05 by the time we actually took the air. I had asked to be towed upwind towards a cloud street over Harrow, but we had barely crossed the aerodrome boundary – only 600 feet up just east of the gasometer – when the aeroplane ahead jumped as if it had been shot. Instinctively I released, then cursed myself for being so hasty.

However, there was undoubtedly lift near by, and after a little searching she took it fairly in the seat of the pants. The variometer jumped from 6 to 9, and a little later to 12 feet per second. We circled up, back over one corner of the aerodrome, into the base of a cloud at 3,600 feet near the Staines reservoir. I turned her nose north-west, put it well down, and struck off at 65 m.p.h. The battle was on.

North of Staines was another cumulus. I found the up-current beneath it at 2,500 feet showing 3 feet per second – but this was not enough. I now declared as a rule of the day that when over 3,000 feet I would not be content with

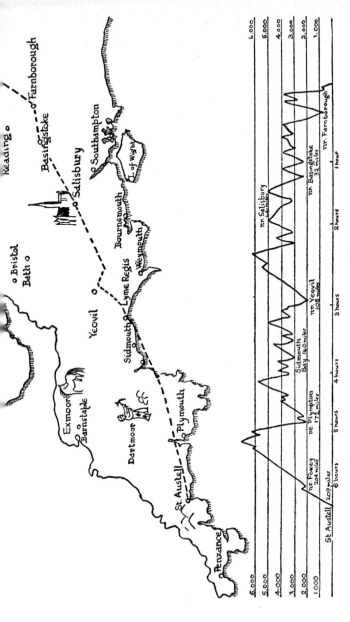

21 *Heston to St Austell*

3 feet per second. If after a search I could not bring it up to at least 5 feet per second, I would go on. But I would never just circle in bovine content unless I got up to 9 feet per second. Until that point was reached I watched every circle, and manœuvred restlessly, searching for the 'meatiest' bits. Time was the essence of the flight, and to save it meant constant hard work. Lesser lift I used by flying through it as slowly as possible, only putting the nose down again when it was past.

I worked this second thermal up to 6 feet per second and then set off again. But this time further lift was hard to find. Virginia Water and Fort Belvedere slid beneath and I was getting dangerously low. I abandoned the cross-wind struggle and went straight downwind towards a large common short of Farnborough (Chobham Ridge). I was miserably reflecting that there was not a safe landing spot in sight, that there was a lot of luck in putting a sailplane down in one piece, and that I had wasted all my work, when suddenly we struck lift! I was 700 feet above my start and perhaps 500 feet above the common below. A last-minute save!

My pride over rates of climb quite gone, we struggled round and round and round. A while later we were up again at 3,900 feet just north of Farnborough, well off course and rather depressed.

However, this was the last shock for a long way. We got back on to our course at Basingstoke, flew along south of the road to Whitchurch, where we worked up a thermal to over 15 feet per second, along to Andover, with Southampton Water and the Isle of Wight in sight, and then Salisbury. The rolling country of the plain was, as expected, stiff with thermals.

Over Salisbury we had some fun. We found ourselves climbing at 6 feet per second up beside a large dense-looking cumulus cloud. The best lift seemed to be in a circle of which the nearest point was perhaps 25 yards south of the wall of cloud. At 5,100 feet this lift declined, so I decided to go inside to try for more. We charged at the solid wall of cloud, hit it, and burst out on the other side as if through a pane of frosted glass. It could not have been more than 25 yards thick; then we were in clear air again in the most violent downdraught of the day – over 15 feet per second.

'You nibble a piece off this side', said Alice, 'and you grow taller: off the other side and grow shorter. Curiouser and curiouser.' I went back and nibbled some more off the other side.

I had been carefully checking my average speed, and found that we had made 32 miles for each of the first two hours. This would get us to the proposed junction with the coast at Lyme Regis at about three o'clock. After that I expected to be able to increase speed. I reckoned on being safe until 3.30, so it might be a near thing to catch Brer Fox, which would take place, if at all, at Exmouth.

But I was wrong in my calculations. The big speed-up of the day was at hand. After passing Salisbury, we flew along the line of hills, past White Sheet Hill, to Shaftesbury, and in this third hour we covered 44 miles. Now came Blackmore Vale, which I had previously found on a flight to Plympton rather cold to strangers. It was once again. As before, near Yeovil, I gave up and turned north to make for the aerodrome. Again I spotted the same little sloping wood which had saved me before, and again it came to my aid. The conditions were extraordinarily similar to the previous occasion from now on to Exmouth.

We climbed thankfully to 3,800 feet, and then made no bones about it by fairly bolting downwind for the sea. Between Bridport and Lyme Regis was the same belt of coastal lift – formed from one to three miles out to sea by a south-easterly sea breeze under-cutting the north-easter. In this way we flew fast along the coast, over the blue sea, past Seaton, Babbacombe, Sidmouth, to Exmouth. Here the same strong thermal took us up to 5,500 feet, and after my last experience at this spot a new caution beset me. Our ground-speed had increased greatly since reaching the coast, as I had expected. But the struggle at Yeovil had brought the fourth hour's kill down to 32 miles again. We put our first bird, Exmouth, in the bag and concentrated on the second – Plymouth.

The wind was now dropping, the clouds dissolving. From Exmouth we flew to a cloud beyond Newton Abbot, where I found an unexpected aerodrome. Weak lift from a seedy-looking thermal took us slowly to 4,000 feet again, and then a long glide found us heading down a river ending in an estuary and a cardboard conical island planted in its mouth – Bigbury. The fifth hour again saw 32 miles go by.

The prospect of getting enough height to cross the high land to the north and making Plymouth aerodrome seemed remote, although as we crossed one or two of the brown, rocky spurs of Dartmoor with perhaps 500 feet to spare, I found weak lift over each. With a prevailing dearth of landing-grounds, I was thinking of making a bid for the beach at Bigbury, so recently furrowed by the skid of the 'Sperber, when we came to the end of Dartmoor.

Just to the north I saw the text-book spot for a wind-shadow thermal. Dartmoor billowed down from about 1,600 feet in a series of rounded slopes facing the westering sun. The bulk of the moor to the north-east provided obvious protection against the north-east wind. So the quiet air over the slopes should have had every opportunity to warm up. I gave up my safety-first plan of Bigbury sands and reached a hopeful spot at 1,900 feet. Immediately I found lift – in no time Plymouth aerodrome was in the bag. A bit later I began to be torn between completing a 178-mile goal flight or going on while the going was good and trying for 200 miles – a nice round figure. Then I remembered the Golden 'C' requirement – 300 kilometres or 186 miles. By this time I was at cloud base 6,000 feet over Plymouth. Inside the cloud, lift was strong but patchy, and at 6,900 feet I gave up the mental struggle and went on west. I came out of the side of the cloud and saw the irregular coastline of Cornwall ahead – the numerous inlets and rivers silver against the declining sun, the colours of the landscape darkening by silhouette.

I flew along the coast, finding dying lift here and there. The land and sea breezes both seemed to have gone. Smoke below was rising gently and vertically. Six hours – and yet again 32 miles covered.

Over the river running down to Fowey was again gentle lift. Farther on I could see St Austell, a surprisingly large town, the hills behind it dotted with huge white pyramids of china clay. I reached it at about 1,500 feet, saw a sloping field behind a garage on a bypass, and circled down to a landing at 5.15 p.m.

I had caught a heavy cold and felt extremely ill. I had had nothing to eat since 8 a.m. But the task of keeping at bay the ravening hordes of small children until the Minimoa was safely packed away took another two hours.

The official distance by great circle course was 209 miles.

11

BRINGING THEM BACK ALIVE

Dream Lady: Back in Chapter One, I offered to become a member of your retrieving team. But so far you haven't told me what I shall have to do.

Me: Ah! That's because I wanted to get in a little more propaganda first. Because what you have suggested tackling is a considerable job: indeed, it has often seemed to me that to the orthodox Proofs of the Existence of a Benevolent Deity should now be added the remarkable fact that He has created a small but priceless percentage of human beings who are prepared to take on, without reward, the arduous labours of ground team to a sailplane pilot.

Many private owners of sailplanes solve the difficulty by sharing their aircraft. Indeed, this is also a good solution to the financial problem, because although there are comparatively few who can these days afford all to themselves a slap-up modern high-performance sailplane with all trimmings complete, there are a number who, in a syndicate of three or four pilots, can manage the proportionate cost; and whilst one flies, the others retrieve. But the fortunate few who can both afford their own aircraft and find someone prepared to chase them all over the globe have a tremendous advantage.

Now, as for the size of the job – but are you sure you are feeling quite well?

D.L.: Yes, perfectly well, thank you. Tell me the worst.

Me: Well, I have been gliding now for about twenty years, and in that time I reckon that the existing Permanent Member of my retrieving team has motored after me, with trailer, about 85,000 miles, or around three and a half times round the globe.

D.L.: Oh Lord! So, if I take it on, how can I be sure of being here to welcome back my husband from his caving expeditions?

Me: You can't, I fear. And so, dear Dream Lady, it is time to wake up. But maybe you have heard enough to try and tempt him to transfer his intelligible enthusiasm for exploring holes in the ground to the surely equally intelligible fascination of exploring the air. If so, we may meet again.

D.L.: Well, maybe. But, in case this happens, tell me, before you go, what I should have to do.

A full team, achievable only in competition work, should consist of three people in addition to the pilot. All must be really skilled at driving with the trailer; at least one should be good at carrying out repairs to the aircraft, in the event of minor damage; and one skilled in car maintenance and, if fitted, the maintenance of the radio stations in car and aircraft. All must be good at map-reading. But the basic member of the ground team, without whom nothing can happen, is the driver.

The first job in the morning, after arrival at the site, is to assemble the sailplane from its trailer. Machines differ greatly in ease of rigging, and many designers have paid too little attention to this feature. The German Weihe is perhaps the best machine ever designed from this aspect, and three practised people can have her out of her trailer and fully rigged in less than 10 minutes. This involves getting out the fuselage, both wings, and the tailplane, and assembling all four units. The Weihe is the more remarkable in that it is a large machine, of nearly 60-feet span, and so the units are necessarily fairly large and heavy. However, it is a pre-war design, and has now been outclassed in other ways by later aircraft, notably by our British Slingsby Sky.

After rigging, the aircraft has to be checked over and towed to the take-off point; then the pilot has to be got in, with his parachute, maps, food and drink, oxygen mask and barographs, after which he is finally launched.

Before take-off he has decided on his task and briefed his retrieving team accordingly. The reader will by now have grasped (if he didn't know it already) that a sailplane flight is a very much more controlled affair than is popularly supposed, and even if the pilot has decided to go for maximum distance, although he will not know his actual landing spot he will know the general direction that his flight will take. If possible, on a distance flight he will fly directly downwind in order to achieve the highest possible average ground-speed during the hours of thermal activity.

In competition flying, with contest-flying every day, it is obviously of cardinal importance for his team to reach their pilot, pick him up, and get him back to base at the earliest possible moment, so that he can get in as much sleep as possible before the next day's flying. With bad luck, or a lazy team, a pilot may find himself flying all day and driving back all night for several days on end; and the time will quickly arrive when he will be beaten by sheer physical exhaustion.

This is why radio-telephonic communication between car and sailplane is so tremendous an asset, since with this aid it is quite possible for the ground-team to keep so close to their sailplane that they may be actually waiting in the field when their pilot lands.

Without radio this is obviously impossible; but even so, I have been picked up after a flight of 150 miles within an hour of landing.

The pilot's general direction of flight being decided before take-off, the car and trailer set off in this direction as soon as their sailplane is in the air and has succeeded in finding lift and 'getting away'. Two drivers go in the car, while the third stays behind and rests, starting a system of rotation for the drivers. Every hour, if weather conditions look diffi-cult, or every two hours if not, the retrievers stop and tele-phone back to base for news of their pilot: if none has come through, they drive on. Immediately the pilot lands, he hurries to the nearest telephone and reports his exact where-abouts to base. This information is then passed on to his team when next they phone through.

Since the average cross-country speed of a sailplane, on a light-wind day with medium lift, may be under 30 m.p.h., devoted retrievers can nearly keep up with their aircraft in favourable country, if they forswear stops for food, drink, or any of the pleasures of life.

It will be seen, however, that this system presupposes a fairly thickly populated country with adequate road and telephone communications. In their absence a pilot may be limited to flying always within range of a main road, to avoid the possibility of being lost for hours or even days.

Having found their pilot, the aircraft is de-rigged and put into the trailer, and the race back to base begins. It is a great advantage if the car is of the Utility type, to permit the pilot to lie down in the back and doze on the way home, whilst the two team members take it in turn to drive.

From the above it will be seen that retrieving is much like a large-scale egg-and-spoon race, the pilot being the privileged egg, and the trailer, whose length is half the span of the glider – 30 feet in the case of a 60-foot span machine – the long-handled spoon.

Trailers can be of many kinds, from crude open frameworks on an old car axle to miniature hangars on wheels. For serious work, a proper weather-proof and (in dusty countries) dust-proof trailer is an essential. It must be painted a light colour, preferably silver, to reflect back the sun's rays, otherwise it will become in hot sunlight an oven which will quickly bake the moisture out of the plywood of the sailplane inside, which then loses much of its strength.

Although driving a glider trailer is less difficult than it looks, providing one has an adequate car, it is not possible to take too many precautions against the risk of tow-bar failure. I know nothing more terrifying than to have a loose 30-foot trailer thundering along out of control behind you. A stout check-rope, attached to the trailer chassis at some strong point and looped through the rear end of each back spring of the car, is enough to enable the driver to keep directional control of the trailer should it break away. This is a Must.

The trailer axle and the machine inside should be so positioned that the trailer is between 30 lb. and 40 lb. nose-heavy, both empty and with the glider aboard. This is about the maximum weight that a single person can cope with when hitching up. If it is nose-heavier than this, it becomes a burden to manhandle; if lighter, a trailer is apt to 'snake' when towed at speed or in a cross-wind. In bad cases, a 'snake' can end up in a 'jack-knife', when the entire trailer swings round and forwards, ending up with one side crushing the side of the car. If anyone were to be coming the other way when this happens, the consequences could obviously be grave indeed. So a good, roadworthy and handy trailer is an absolute essential.

Retrieving stories are as many and various as fishing stories. One of the most famous concerns two brothers who shared a sailplane, taking turn and turn about to fly and retrieve. Charles had departed on a distance flight in a south-easterly direction, Lawrence was dreamily cruising along the road with the empty trailer in the same general direction, with another hour to go before he was due to telephone back to base for any message.

A young lady thumbed for a lift, and Lawrence obligingly stopped. She got in and they drove off, he still musing about gliding matters. After a few minutes' silence, his passenger's curiosity got the better of her, and she burst out: 'What on earth have you got in that enormous trailer?' Her driver looked at her mistily for a moment or two, then absently replied: 'Nothing!' and relapsed into his dream.

After a few minutes to recover, she tried again, more nervously this time: 'Well, where are you going with it?'

'I don't know,' came the reply. This, though strictly truthful, was perhaps a little unfair. It reduced the lady to a terrified silence which was only broken when, in the centre of the next town with a policeman safely in sight, she asked firmly to be put down.

World Gliding Championships take place every other year, and in 1952 were held in Madrid. We had, after each meeting, endeavoured to learn by our failures, and on this occasion had prepared for every eventuality. Amongst other things, we had arranged to arrive ten days before the actual start of the Championships, in order to get in some practice flying over the actual terrain. This is one of those flights.

Madrid is a city rising suddenly out of the plain, of high, hard stone, great buildings of semi-skyscraper appearance. Cuatro Vientos is nine kilometres to the south-west, a huge, brown, dusty aerodrome, with the magnificent buildings and swimming-pool of the Real Aero-Club de España on the south side. We were one of the early arrivals, but as each day passed more and more trailers arrived and familiar faces reappeared from all over the world, as at Örebro and Samaden. The gliding enthusiast would find it difficult to be friendless or lonely in any country of the world today.

We arrived at midday on Saturday 21st June, under a sky I fear I may never see again. It was regularly spotted in every direction with cells of cumulus based at perhaps 8,000 feet, and apart from a wandering surface wind of obviously thermal origin, the upper air was horizontally motionless. It looked as though the world out-and-return record could have been broken by any competent pilot with ease, but we had arrived too late to try. The next two days, however, were nearly as good, so on the fourth I decided to attempt it.

Gliding flights can be divided into two categories: (a) successes, and (b) failures. Ninety-nine per cent of flights come under (b), which can in turn be subdivided into (i) worth while, (ii) miserable, and – again about ninety-nine per cent of the whole subdivision – (iii) just ordinary, run-of-the-mine failures.

This flight had, I think, some fragments of each sub-heading. It was worth while because we tried out a new technique of radio-controlled turning-point. It was run-of-the-mine because I had to land at my turning-point. And it was miserable because I damaged my machine in landing, sheer luck alone confining the accident to one involving only minor repairs. How nearly I ditched my chances of flying in the Championships at all, I don't like to think.

On the part of my retrieving team, it was even (iv) a gallant failure, because they became unwittingly involved in something between a Marathon obstacle race and the Grand Prix d'Europe in their efforts to keep in radio touch with me as I flew along the course.

The plan of operation hinged upon our Pye car-to-air-craft radio sets. By carrying an official observer in the car itself, any suitable turning-point can be chosen and declared at the very last moment, which need not necessarily be an aerodrome. Nor need any elaborate observer arrangement be put in hand before take-off.

All that is required (note the word 'all') is a turning-point decision before take-off, and for the car then to set off and beat the glider to it. The glider arrives overhead, the official observer is awakened from his sound sleep, the pilot radios down 'Here I am – can you see me?' the O.O. yawns 'Yes' and goes off to sleep again, and everyone goes home happy. Or, at least, that was the plot. The official observer concerned, and even more my team, are now in a strong position to say that it is not quite as easy as it sounds – but it is possible.

I launched at 12.20, and the daily cumulus started forming at about 12.40, by which time I was over Madrid at 5,000 feet. The plan was to fly along the main road to Zaragoza, in a direction north by east, to a point 200 kilometres away just short of Calatayud, and back again.

As I circled in my first thermal over Cuatro Vientos, the sky suddenly filled with friendly voices. The rest of the

British team were arriving from home, down the road from the north, led by Ann Douglas in her trailerless car. Reaching the aerodrome first, Ann was trying hard to explain to those following how to negotiate the complications of Madrid. As the other cars and trailers plunged into the high-walled streets, their voices deteriorated into gabbles and clucks for all the world like a farmyard in distress. A while later, they became clear again. 'The bridge on to the Toledo road is blocked. Where do I go from here?' – 'Try the one signposted "Extremadura and Portugal".' – 'Lorne is behind with trailer trouble.' – 'We are stopping at the Hotel Derby – D-E-R-B-Y.'

I set off east, and gradually the ether became again the private property of 'Justin' (the call-sign of my trailer) and 'Philip'.

By the time, however, that 'Justin' emerged on my side of Madrid I was approaching Guadalajara, 50 kilometres on, and my average ground-speed was working up to 65 kilometres an hour, with lift of over 15 feet a second under each cloud. It thus became clear that the only course, which we had discussed before the start, was for 'Justin' to abandon the trailer by the roadside and press on with all possible speed.

The next few hours in the Vanguard must have been a nightmare. Every quarter of an hour or so I reported my position ahead of the car. From Torija to Torresaviñan the Zaragoza road runs straight as a sword across the high, flat plain, and along this the speedometer needle seldom went below 80 m.p.h. The temperature rose with the sun, until it was over 100° F., and in the dry heat the occupants of the car took frequent swigs of Vichy water, which they had great difficulty in getting to their mouths as the car bounded along the not-too-smooth road.

By Alcolea del Pinar I was able to tell them that they were only 5 kilometres behind, but then I saw their road ahead plunge into a range of Sierras, twisting and turning like forty-nine corkscrews.

As they dived madly into this ravine, their voices went out like a light – probably just as well, I thought ruefully, as I sailed easily and quietly in a straight line over the range. By the time they had emerged and were on the air again I had gone a further 20 kilometres ahead, and was loitering for them to catch up. Another 20 kilometres of straight road brought them up again, then a second Sierra, another straight, and a third. This, however, was the last – a few more straight-ish kilometres and the turning-point was to be reached. It was at this precise moment, when their troubles seemed to be over, that I had to report that I had run into an entirely unexpected area of stable air, and might have to land. I have no idea of what caused it – the sun was blazing, I was over a valley with a stream, green borders, dry grey hills on all sides, everything the most choosy thermal might desire. But none was to be found. Ahead was Calatayud, with its extraordinary ruined castle looking down on it from a grey cliff honeycombed with caves, at the mouth of a further defile.

The fields below me were all tiny, but on the farther outskirts of the town was an enormous military barracks, and outside its walls was what looked like a gigantic football field. It was only afterwards that I realised that football fields are roughly the same size everywhere, and this one merely looked large in comparison with all the surrounding fields. I told 'Justin' where I was proposing to land, and how to get there.

All would have been well but for the fact that, in that climate, the surface of the field was as hard and flat as a ballroom floor. Consequently we touched down and ran half the length (and the second half at that) on our skid before stopping, within ten feet of destruction, in a swing which damaged the port wing – but fortunately slightly.

A thousand soldiers arrived, and an officer looked somewhat incredulous when I produced on him the one Spanish sentence which I had learnt up before leaving England – 'My wife will arrive in a blue car in five minutes.' He looked still more startled when she did.

She and the official observer caked with dust, the bonnet of the car streaked with red rust-spots where the radiator had boiled over, there we were in Calatayud with a damaged glider, the trailer 200 kilometres away, 4 p.m., a tired, hot, and above all thirsty party. But we were met with typical Spanish hospitality, beer, soap and water, a garage for the machine beside a row of army lorries, and the task of sorting it all out and getting everything together in one place again. Which makes another saga, but one in general outline unnecessary to tell to all who sail the skies or still more to the heroic band who Get Them Back.

12

THE INSTRUMENT BOARD

When I started to glide, instruments were thought to be rather unsporting. The true pilot was expected to fly by achieving the instincts of a bird as nearly as possible: from the feel of the wind on his face, and the sound of the wind over the wings and fuselage of his machine. For a time, we flew in stockinged feet, without shoes, on the theory that in this way we could manipulate the rudder with greater sensitivity. Personally I gave this up after landing one day, a mile from the nearest road, in a field of thistles. Sensitive feet are all very well to a certain point.

Unfortunately there are several objections to this undoubtedly poetic idea. In the first place, as has been already described on page 58, the construction of the ear of a bird is the reverse of that of a man, and provides him with the most essential of all soaring instruments – a rate-of-climb indicator. In the second place, the modern glider pilot wants to do what a bird never does, and fly where a bird cannot fly – in cloud, without any visual horizon. Thirdly, the soaring pilot scorns an engine, whereas the bird has at his disposal plenty of motive power to get him out of tight corners. So we called science to our aid, and with science came instruments which, after all, are essentially extensions to one's senses.

Anyone who looks at the instrument panel of a modern sailplane will realise how very out-of-date it would make Lilienthal or the Wright brothers feel.

1 The Altimeter, indicating altitude, simply measures the pressure of the air above it by means of a vacuum capsule, as contained in a weather barometer, which does exactly the same thing only less so.

2 The Air-Speed Indicator (A.S.I.) does what its name implies. The needle is coupled to a diaphragm, one side of which is coupled to the static tube of the pitot head which is closed in front, with small holes drilled in the side, and the other side to the open pitot head. The pressure of the air on this open tube as the machine flies forwards varies, of course, with the speed, and is registered by the needle on the dial of the instrument.

The external pitot head has certain disadvantages. On the ground it has an irresistible attraction for small boys, who blow down it whenever one's attention wanders: this completely wrecks an expensive instrument. Furthermore, it is an excrescence from the smooth streamline of the fuselage, and so has an adverse, if small, effect on performance. Lastly, it attracts ice-formation, and is frequently blocked by ice just when most needed, when the pilot is flying blind in turbulent cloud. This can be ameliorated by heating it electrically.

2a Pitot head heating switch.

3 The Variometer, or rate-of-climb indicator, is the cardinal instrument of the soaring pilot. As a machine climbs, air-pressure decreases. The *rate at which the air-pressure decreases* is therefore related to the rate of climb. So we need an instrument which will show, immediately, rates of climb and descent of as little as six inches a second, and up to 20 feet a second and more. When one tries to imagine the minute difference in the atmospheric pressure on, say, this page you are reading and on your eye reading it from about a foot above, it seems a fantastic requirement

that an instrument be provided which will register if lifted slowly, in two seconds, from book to eye. Yet it has been met, and the British instrument used weighs only about 2 ounces and is virtually unbreakable and everlasting.

A pint thermos flask contains a reservoir of air which is insulated from heat and cold, which might otherwise affect its volume. If it is moved up or down, a minute amount of air leaks out of or into it. It is connected to the variometer in such a way that air flowing out has to pass up a slightly tapered transparent plastic tube, sealed at its base by a hollow perspex green ball. To get out, the air has to lift the ball. The faster one climbs, the faster the air escapes, and the higher it lifts the ball.

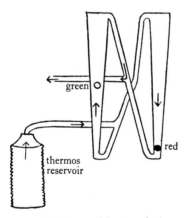

22   *Variometer (showing climb)*

On descending, air gets into the thermos through a second tube sealed by a red ball, which it lifts in the same way. Each ball registers against a scale, from which the pilot can read his rate of climb or descent.

This is the simple variometer, but modern practice has produced two recent and very important improvements. One has already been referred to in Chapter 9. By attaching cruise-speed charts to the variometer, a pilot can read off the correct speeds at which he must fly in different wind and thermal conditions, either to achieve maximum range, or to achieve maximum speeds. The cruise-speed chart is the white vertical slip along the left-hand edge of the instrument.

The second, and most ingenious improvement of all, was first devised by H. Kendall, who called it the Total Energy variometer. This instrument no longer shows if the *machine* is losing or gaining height, it actually shows whether the *air* in which the machine is flying is rising or descending, even if the pilot is diving or climbing his machine at the time. Even in a loop, the Total Energy variometer will show 'Red' all the way round.

This new instrument has created tremendous interest in high-performance circles. It gave me a Secret Weapon which helped me greatly to victory in the 1952 World Championships. It is desirable to fit an ordinary variometer as a reserve instrument, as well, as an insurance against icing risks.*

4 The Turn-and-Bank Indicator is a necessity for blind flying, when, as will be described later, human senses become, in the absence of any visual reference to the horizon, actually misleading.

One needle of this instrument is a simple pendulum, which actually shows skid or slip. The second is coupled to a gyroscope, which in the special instrument used in sail-

* A full description of the functioning and design of the Total Energy Variometer is contained in *Gliding*, Vol. III, Nos. 1 & 2. This is the official journal of the British Gliding Association, 19 Park Lane, W.1.

planes is electrically spun from torch batteries. It registers yaw – the rate at which the aircraft is turning in the plane of the wing-surfaces. (Yaw is only equivalent to 'right' or 'left' when the machine is on a level keel. In a vertical bank, yaw – the effect produced by the application of rudder – becomes 'up' or 'down'. The pupil pilot has reached an important milestone when he has absorbed this point – the interchangeability of controls.)

Being electrically driven, this instrument has to be shielded if radio is also carried, to avoid interference. It is a complicated and necessarily expensive instrument compared with the others, but the British type is beautifully reliable.

In early days, turn-and-bank indicators were driven by an external venturi tube protruding from the side of the fuselage. But this invariably iced up in big clouds, when the instrument was most needed, and was accordingly a highly dangerous device, since it tempted one into cloud and then failed.

When flying blind, the pilot has to read simultaneously the turn-and-bank, A.S.I., and variometer, so these instruments should be grouped together, preferably in the centre of the panel.

4a Turn-and-Bank Indicator switch.

5 Compass. An ordinary small aircraft magnetic compass is used. It is liable to error when the turn-and-bank indicator is switched on, so should be mounted away from it though this is not always possible.

6 Oxygen Panel. This instrument reduces the pressure in the oxygen bottle (which is stowed behind the pilot's seat) from the full pressure of over 2,000 lb. per square inch, and feeds it to the oxygen mask, which is slipped on by the pilot when required.

7 Quick-Release Knob. When pulled, this operates the quick-release, and so drops the towing cable.

8 Airbrake Operating Lever. (Usually similar in position and direction of operation to an aeroplane throttle lever.)

9 Undercarriage Release Knob. Most high-performance sailplanes are launched on a small two-wheeled trolley, which is dropped off once the aircraft is airborne.

10 Trimmer Operating Knob. This operates a small flap on the trailing edge of one elevator, which enables the pilot to trim his machine to fly at a set speed, hands off the controls.

11 Ventilator Knob. When flying in rain, hail or extreme cold, it is very necessary for the cockpit to be well sealed, so that the pilot can remain dry and reasonably warm. This results in much condensation on the inside of the cockpit cover, and this freezes at altitude and reduces the pilot's range of vision to nil.

A ventilator in the nose and a small opening panel or window in the hood itself keeps sufficient cold air flowing through the cockpit to keep the hood clear. But at great altitudes the cold becomes so severe that the pilot must keep everything shut, and occasionally scratch a hole in the frosted inside surface of his hood as a look-out.

For constant flying at great altitudes, satisfactory clear-vision panels have been designed which do not frost up, and these are used, with electrically heated clothing and what-have-you, for wave exploration. But such special equipment is outside the scope of this book.

The remaining instrument is a recording barograph. Most people have a comfortable uncle with a recording barometer ticking away in the hall, drawing a purple line on a revolving drum. The recording barograph is the same instrument, but the line indicates altitude instead of barometric pressure. Recording barographs can have a rough life, and have been known to fail, and so it is wise to carry two. Two of my best height flights have been vitiated by barograph failures.

If fitted, the radio set is carried next to the oxygen bottle, behind the pilot's seat. As used in the 1952 Championships it was switched on before take-off and left on all the time. The pilot wore a single headphone, and used a hand microphone. A small bicycle-type brake-lever handle was fitted on the stick, and operated when it was desired to transmit. It was not possible to receive and transmit simultaneously. Range is limited to line-of-sight, and so increases with altitude. From 5,000 feet a range of 50 miles was frequently exceeded. When the car is in city streets, shielded by buildings, or in mountain passes, the radio becomes practically inoperative.

This is the sort of flight that is a good deal nearer the real thing than the ones that usually get into print; but if you like reading sentences like: 'I had long lost sight of the green ball, and thought that it might have burst its way out of the top of the tube,' or: 'Brussels was now in sight, and I had to decide whether to land and net the goal-flight record, or to carry on for a stab at the World's distance' – if you like that sort of thing (and very nice too), well, skip this.

Once Upon a Time I visited one of our West Country clubs. One evening the forecast promised light westerlies and reasonably good instability. So we hatched a plot. From the Club aerodrome to the Norfolk coast wasn't far enough for a distance record, so we planned an aero-tow over to Wales, and a release somewhere north of Swansea. From there to the seaside gave a downwind run of around 250 miles, which was enough.

So, far into the night, we pored over maps and worked out courses and times, and drew enormous straight lines with the aid of the marble top of the hotel washstand. Came the dawn, a cloudless blue with a touch of haze.

By 9.30 we were at the aerodrome: the trailer was out. We rigged, and by 10.15 were on the tarmac. The tug was refuelling, my wife getting the sandwiches. No cumulus were yet forming.

By 10.30 the tug had arrived, and we found that everybody had thought someone else was getting the tow-rope. Someone went for it, and the tug stopped its engine. By 10.45 the tow-rope was fetched and laid out. By 11.00 I was in, with two sealed barographs. Then someone realised that the tug-pilot needed a third, so we waited whilst one was found, set and sealed. My sandwiches were tucked in beside my right knee, my maps by my left knee; in my breast-pocket were my boiled sweets, a handkerchief, my sunglasses and a tube of benzedrine to sniff if my sinus gave trouble in rapid descents from great heights. I was strapped in, the tug started its engine.

My oxygen mask was strapped round my neck and I plugged in the tube and turned it on for a test. Nothing happened: I had forgotten to unscrew the tap on the bottle, which is *behind the seat*!

I sent a message to the tug to stop its engine (I didn't want it to have to go and refuel again); I was unstrapped. My sandwiches, maps, barographs and gloves were taken out and I undid my parachute and got out. I lifted the seat forward and turned on the oxygen. I put my parachute on again, got in, was fitted in with all the bits and pieces enumerated above. Someone shut the cockpit-cover – right away? The ring was put into the quick-release, the wing-tip holder lifted his tip, the signaller waved his flag. . . The tug-pilot, with a resigned look on his distant but by now rather red face, beckoned for help. He wanted someone to swing his prop . . .

A volunteer trotted out to the Tiger. . . After he was worn out, we sent a second, then a third. The Gipsy engine, having registered its merited protest at our goings-on, came to reluctant life, not before – in my cockpit under the glare of the sun – my face, already somewhat red, had finally assumed the moist scarlet of boiled lobster.

11.20 . . . it was getting rather late, but still no cu. Tighten up . . . the aircraft crept forward, the rope tightened – all out! Slowly we rolled forward, the somewhat derisive faces of my long-suffering helpers and watchers dropped behind, the wing-tip trotter trotted, ran, let go. We trundled along the runway, lifted.

By now my reasoning powers were almost suspended. I pulled the undercart release to drop my wheels. With a slight twang the tow-rope came off – I had pulled the wrong knob. . .

We landed back on the runway which we had left after so much toil, and came to rest. The tug had had to go on and take off. It was crossing the aerodrome boundary, climbing. But it didn't turn left to make a circuit and land again. It went on and on in a straight line, climbing away towards Wales. It got higher and higher and smaller and smaller, and vanished over the horizon.

My disillusioned team arrived to tow me back, and we looked at each other for a long minute. Then we all decided to laugh. We laughed and laughed. I unstrapped myself and got out, carelessly showering maps and sandwiches on the runway all round. We lay down in the shade of the wing and

143

laughed until we felt better. Then we towed the machine back to the clubhouse and had a few drinks.

An hour later the tug arrived back, and its demoralised pilot confessed that he had never before towed anything smaller than a Horsa. He had not therefore been surprised at the brisk rate of climb of his Tiger, and had not thought to look back until he had reached our Welsh rendezvous.

He was feeling rather foolish until he was told why I had come detached, then he realised that he was only running second in the Pilot Prune stakes.

Anyway, the day never did boil up, and there wasn't a record to be had. So we went home. But I think I had some claim to at least one World's record – the Shortest Flight ever achieved in a record attempt. In setting out to do 250 miles, I must have covered all of 200 yards.

A Slingsby Sky sailplane.

Sailplanes and their trailers at the 1950 sailplane championships at Örebro, Sweden.

13

COMPETITION FLYING

There are various kinds of tasks a pilot may set himself to achieve, and national and international records are recognised in the following:

Distance in a straight line.

Goal flight, to a landing-point declared by the pilot before take-off.

Out-and-return flight, round a turning-point declared by the pilot before take-off.

Gain of height.

Absolute altitude achieved above sea-level.

Duration.

Speed over a triangular course of 100 kilometres.

In addition, a task set in competition flying is a race to a point laid down by the organisers.

These records are split into two categories, single-seat sailplanes and multi-seaters, and there is an additional class for feminine records in each category. Personally I disapprove of this. I am sufficiently a feminist to hold that the ladies can make pilots every bit as good as the opposite sex, indeed I had irrefutable proof of this in Air Transport Auxiliary when over a hundred women pilots, ferrying all types of military aircraft, put up records of competence and safety indistinguishable from the men. And indeed world gliding records have at times been held by a woman pilot, although whilst she was holding them there was no outcry from the men that there should be established masculine records. But perhaps I should tiptoe on.

Distance flying (unrestricted). The general technique for this type of flying has already been covered in previous chapters.

Goal flying. To determine before take-off the most distant point which you think you can reach, and then to land within one kilometre of this point, is a stern discipline. It involves very careful examination of the latest available weather information and of the map, to decide in which direction the best flying conditions are likely to be met.

When the goal has been decided, the course you intend to follow should be ruled clearly on the map. It is a good idea to mark off this line every 25, 50, 75, 100 etc., kilometres (or miles) from the point of take-off, so that one can quickly check the distance covered at hourly intervals, and so determine one's average speed.

Thermal conditions in summer in England seldom persist for longer than seven or eight hours – say from 11 a.m. to 6.30 p.m. on a good day – and therefore the distance away of the goal you set yourself should be the anticipated duration of the flight multiplied by the estimated average speed you hope to achieve.

If you underestimate the conditions, you reach your goal with good useful flying hours still available, which are wasted since the goal flight is vitiated if you overfly your declared landing-point.

A perfect goal flight is achieved when you just reach your goal with a few hundred feet to spare, after a long glide at maximum-range speed from the top of the very last thermal of the day. This is the experience of a lifetime – I have only achieved it once.

Out-and-return flight. This is, in effect, a flight to a goal, and then a return flight to the point of take-off. It is even more difficult to achieve optimum results on a given day, than in the case of a one-way goal flight. When attempting such a flight, one problem is to ensure that a suitable official on the ground shall see the glider arrive and circle the turning-point at a considerable altitude, since the machine cannot risk descending too low and losing the lift.

As we saw in Chapter 1 it is almost impossible for a ground observer to detect and locate a soundless aircraft flying high overhead. He cannot lie on his back for long periods, scanning the dazzling sky above.

My wife and I solved this problem in the following way. An aerodrome is selected for the turning-point, and from my estimated average speed I calculate how many hours it will take me to reach it after 'getting away'. When she sees me achieve this, she waits for the agreed lapse of time, and then telephones the control officer at the aerodrome selected. She then tells him, in effect, 'Please go to the window, and overhead you will see a sailplane circling. Please then fire a green Very light at it and come back and confirm that I am right.'

The observer either comes back to the 'phone and says, in a surprised voice, that the machine is there, or else that it is not. In the latter case, she rings off, but phones again half an hour later with the same request. If the sailplane fails to reach the turning-point, one ends up with one more dis-illusioned control-tower officer. If it does, it has to circle round the aerodrome until the next half-hour strikes, when, on seeing the green light, the pilot knows he has been marked, and turns for home.

An out-and-return flight is obviously easiest in conditions of no wind, which are rare in this country. When such days do arrive, haze is only too likely to cut off the heat of the sun and so reduce thermal strength. If there is any wind, either both legs must be flown across wind, or one downwind and the return leg against wind, which will greatly reduce the achievable average speed.

Gain of height. This is defined as the greatest height achieved during a flight minus the lowest height reached *previously* in free flight. To make this clear, suppose one is aero-towed and releases at 2,000 feet, and then descends to 1,000 feet before finding lift in which one climbs to 10,000 feet. The gain of height achieved is 9,000 feet.

Absolute altitude is the maximum height achieved during a flight *above sea-level*, irrespective of the height of launch. No absolute altitude performance is recognised unless, during the flight, there is a *gain of height* of at least 5,000 metres (approximately 16,500 feet).

Duration. Duration flying is not rated very high in these days. There are parts of the world where the wind blows from one direction for weeks on end, and from a hill facing such a wind, duration flying becomes a matter more of the endurance of the human frame than the skill of the human mind.

Speed over a 100-kilometre triangular course. This is a goal race round two turning-points and back to the point of take-off. It is a difficult task, and requires exceptionally good weather conditions for fulfilment.

Goal race. This is an excellent task, calling for much skill, but being usually of comparatively short duration, not too fatiguing. It also does not put as much strain as does distance flying on the retrieving team.

Since unrestricted distance flying also involves flying as fast as possible, racing requires much the same flying technique, and in Great Britain, where the size of the island rather than the skill of the pilot usually limits distance flights, racing is an excellent substitute to enable him to practise until the day when he gets to a larger country and can let himself go.

Since the goal is laid down for him, the pilot is saved from the agonies of selection, and only has to consider how he can get there in the shortest possible time. One of his trickiest problems is the final glide-in. It is easy to waste much time circling in the final thermal and climbing unnecessarily high, in which case he will arrive in a screaming high-speed dive which advertises his error to all onlookers. It is also easy – and much worse – to start one's final glide-in too soon, and land short of the goal, which loses one nearly all one's marks.

It is a helpful plan, after ruling one's track on the map before take-off, to mark on the last 20 miles or so of the line the safe altitude one must possess at each five-mile interval to be able to reach the goal.

Modern gliding championships consist of setting the pilots a daily task, which they all attempt at the same time. The tasks which may be set are those outlined in the first part of this chapter, with the exception of duration, which is no longer set, and Absolute Altitude, which would in contest flying merely overlap Gain of Height.

Various kinds of marking systems are employed. For instance, if the task is unrestricted distance, a pilot may receive one mark for every mile covered. In the event of a race, he may receive marks equal to, say, five times his average speed over the course. There remains the problem of equating the value of a flight carried out on one day in good weather conditions as against another similar flight on a difficult day. It will require much more skill to fly 50 miles on a bad day than 150 miles on a good one. To equalise this, a Daily Factor is used, whereby the best performance on each day wins, say, 1,000 marks and everyone else's marks are scaled accordingly. To make this clear, suppose that, on a distance day, the best flight is one of 170 miles, gaining 170 marks. This pilot's marks are multiplied by $\frac{1,000}{170}$, giving him 1,000 points. Everyone else's marks on that day are also multiplied by the same Daily Factor.

Competition flying is almost the only way of finding out how good (or bad) a pilot you are; because it is almost the only flying in which you have the yardstick of what other pilots can do when flying against you in the same conditions. When flying on your own you can land at the end of the day and think you have done well – but there is no means of telling that someone else might not have done much better.

There is nothing like competition flying for improving one's technique. It can be exhilarating, depressing, frightening, delirious, exhausting and stimulating in rapid succession. It is living at the summit of experience.

It was the fourth day of the 1948 World Gliding Championships, held at Samaden in Switzerland. At the morning briefing of competitors at 08.30 in the wooden hut on the airfield, the contest for the day was announced as the 100-kilometre triangular race.

No such stiff test had ever before been set a meeting of sailplane pilots. It was widely believed that no one would succeed in completing the course, which, commencing with a dive over the starting line, on the Muottas Murail three thousand feet above the valley floor, involved a flight across the Engadine valley and over a tumbled mass of mountains to the Davos valley, on a course of about 355 degrees magnetic, turning-point the Weissflüjoch at the head of the famous funicular, thence on a course of about 220 degrees along the north-west side of the Davos valley to Piz Curver, and a run home once more over massed mountains rising to over eleven thousand feet on a course of approximately 110 degrees. Total distance, 101 kilometres.

The early day was a perfect cloudless blue, the morning sun shining bright and clear on that unbelievable valley, the green floor of which, flat as a billiard table, is 5,000 feet above sea-level, and which is walled at each side by mountains running from eight thousand to fourteen thousand feet, capped with snow.

At about 11 o'clock the windsock puffed out from the south – the Maloja wind had started to blow. One after another the bright sailplanes were winched up. They turned on to the neighbouring slopes of Muottas Murail, and traversed them to the top. I was off the ground at 11.24. I climbed to 8,000 feet and beat up and down the Pontresina valley, awaiting the beginning of the cumulus.

The steep slope beneath was scarred with parallel walls of rough stone, to break the winter avalanches. Half-way along was a hut, perched on the top, a Swiss flag fluttering languidly from a pole in the beer-garden. As one passed, often level with it, cheerful drinkers would wave. Twenty or more sailplanes traversing that giant beat seemed quite enough, for the lift was narrow and close to the tumbled scree of rock.

At about 12.45 I was sailing near the starting-line, in front of the hotel perched at the head of the funicular, when I saw a streak of gunmetal grey dive down from above, across the valley towards the far slope of Crasta Mora. The first machine was away. A few small flat cumulus had started to form, very high, probably around 17,000 feet. There seemed to be little or no upper wind. The south-westerly Maloja wind is a valley wind and does not go very high.

Indeed, Alpine winds are to me completely incalculable. The south-west Maloja wind in the Engadine valley is sometimes accompanied by a precisely opposite wind in the Davos valley only 30 kilometres away to the north, and whilst both are blowing low down the upper wind may be nil.

I watched the receding dot across the valley, and saw how immediately it reached the far side it started to climb rapidly the razor of Crasta Mora. It was time to go.

23   100 *km. triangular race*

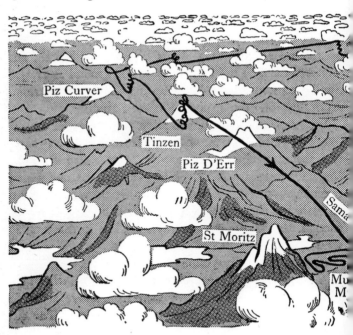

So well had I sealed the Gull IV cockpit, and so strong is the machine, that at 160 kilometres an hour she is rock steady and quieter than the average machine at her normal speed. Across the line I eased her back to 110 kilometres an hour and was across the valley and six kilometres on my course in a few minutes. Strong lift on Crasta Mora immediately took me to 10,000 feet, and now I was faced with a serious decision.

The general view before take-off had been that the best chance of completing the course was to attempt it in a clockwise direction. But to the west towards Piz Curver the cumulus still seemed very sparse, whereas to the north

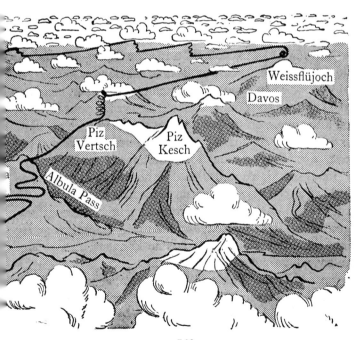

things looked better. I wasted a fatal ten minutes making up my mind, then saw two or three machines over Piz Kesch to the north and above me, so set off in that direction.

There are two ways of tackling an Alpine flight. One is, always to keep a bolt-hole in sight, never cross a mountain without enough height to get either back or on to the next valley, or go round. The other, perhaps only permissible in international contest flying: don't wait. Get on and hope. So far we had not experienced a day which tempted one to the second course, and for this first phase I hung on to the safety line. But gradually I began to realise that this day was unlike any other I had ever dreamed of, and that caution was almost unnecessary.

Leaving Crasta Mora I crossed the Albula Pass to a cloud over Piz Vertsch. Underneath it the green ball rose and rose again till it disappeared in the top of the tube: over 20 feet a second climb! At 12,000 feet I turned on the oxygen, and the lift continued to the base of the thin, flat cloud at 17,000 feet. Now it was just a question of holding a compass course at 110 kilometres an hour until the Davos valley came in sight; on a mountain on the far side was the hotel with a yellow cross marking the turning-point. One had to circle it at not over 1,500 feet, or about 10,000 feet above sea-level.

I was too high and had to dive up to 160 kilometres an hour again to circle it. Then on to the new course, along the edge of the valley, rather nerve-racking now, because if one got down below the crests of the flanking mountains, and so into the valley wind, there was no knowing, in a strange valley, where one could find slope lift.

I passed Lorne Welch, in his Olympia, about half a mile on my left, and south of Arosa, almost level with the mountain tops, found my lift. Lorne, though so near, was just that

much lower to be out of the pure thermal, and later told me
that he had had a bad struggle and lost much time here. But
I was away again, green ball out of sight; into cloud base,
only to find that lift inside was not worth while.

So on to course again, humming through the grey ragged
fringes of the cloud at 110 kilometres an hour, not enough
sight of the mountains below to locate myself, depending
entirely on my compass, and my ability to hold a compass
course on the needles of my turn-and-bank indicator.

Gradually I sank below cloud-base and saw ahead the deep
valley running down to Tiefencastel, where it is joined by
another gigantic valley running down from the Julier Pass.
On the far side was the range of which one spike was Piz
Curver, the next turning-point. But which was it? Alpine
maps are not very clear, and Alpine scenery so fantastic and
tumbled that one peak looks much like the other thousand.
I reached the far side and wasted another precious ten
minutes in finding the yellow cross on the mountainside.

Then on to the home course, once more a nervous few
minutes hoping for lift to the upper atmosphere; but under
the next cloud up she went.

Soon we were again at 17,000 feet on our course; but
when down to 15,000 feet I again found lift near Tinzen, the
question was, to take it or not? Had I height to make the
homeward run in one? I should have worked it out before.
I should have marked distances on each leg, but I hadn't;
and ahead of me lay the highest and wildest mountain mass
of the whole course, the Piz d'Err.

So I took the lift and spent another few minutes rocketing
back to cloud-base, then on. For minute after minute I sat,
flying at 110 kilometres an hour, a whiff of oxygen, a bar of
chocolate, the bright sun and blue sky and clouds overhead,

in every direction below tumbled thousands of white-topped peaks stretching up to the horizon, sliding gently and silently past, in dead smooth, silky air. I never hope again to live through such glory; it was the sailplane pilot's idea of Elysium.

Then the last peak dropped, and ahead I saw again the Engadine valley, and on the far side, the hotel at the top of the mountain wall. I had too much height, I needn't have used that last thermal after all. I pushed up the speed to 145 kilometres an hour, flashed across the valley past the hotel in a 180° turn, and the white line rushed below at 170 kilometres an hour; time, 14.58.38 hrs. Then I was over the edge again looking down on the airfield three thousand feet below. Airbrakes on, we screamed down to a landing.

Two hours, 6 minutes, 48 seconds. Any good? Well, Maurer had done it in 1 hour 40 minutes and was off on a second lap! I tottered out of the cockpit, rushed for a cup of chocolate, felt very old, and took off again. But I didn't get far: the conditions were dying and I came back again.

Maurer's second lap was done in 1 hr. 36 min., a world record: mine was still a British record.

Of the 27 starters on this formidable flight no less than 25 completed the course, and I came in eighth. But what a day!

Lessons? Several, but the main one is: Mark off the course, with accurate magnetic bearings on each leg, and mark each leg off in say, 10-kilometre sections. Then one can tell whether at any given point one has enough height to make the next turning-point without waste of time in further lift. The other lessons are probably only applicable on a perfect day such as this in the High Alps, or in Paradise.

14

TO MAIDEN AUNTS

This chapter is not, may I say at once, addressed to the Maiden Aunts of real life, who in my experience are amongst the most plucky and hardworking of all sections of the community.

When a bomb destroyed a London house during the blitz, it was a four-to-one chance that the unhappy occupant trapped inside would be dragged out within a very few minutes by someone's maiden aunt, arriving at least a hundred yards ahead of everyone else. And, having fished him out, and directed him to the nearest cup of tea, as likely as not she would immediately disappear back into the burning building to rescue his cat trapped on the third floor.

No, I am referring to the highly imaginary maiden aunt of fiction – a delicate, nervous lady with fluttering white hands and a triangle of lace over her thin grey hair, always trying to stop her nephews and nieces from doing anything more dangerous than playing with a diabolo: a creature of fiction who seems to me to be a fiction indeed.

Is it safe?

Most enthusiasts trying to snare new recruits to their particular fanaticism seem incapable of giving an objective reply to this question. Indeed, in their very enthusiasm they appear to persuade themselves that gliding – or motor-racing, or ski-ing – is indeed safer than, say, stamp-collecting. Let me say at once that this is not so.

But the very words 'safety' and 'danger' are so charged with emotion, when applied to those you love, that the questioner really fails to understand what they mean. Well, what *do* they mean? What *is* safe?

Is driving a car safe? You can answer this question with a wealth of figures. You can say that statistics show that there is only one fatal accident in 20,000,000 miles' motoring (or whatever it is) in the British Isles. But this is quite a phoney argument if applied to your ancient Uncle George, who is around 85 with the spirit – but not the reaction times – of a boy and always drives flat out down narrow Devonshire lanes. And it is misleading if applied equally to Smith, who drives 2,000 miles a year, and Jones, who drives 15,000 miles in the same time.

You are a little nearer a meaningful answer if you say that if on the railways there is only one accident every 120,000,000 miles, motoring is six times more dangerous on the average than is travelling by rail. But your fictional maiden aunt is not concerned with average necks, but with the neck of dear William – such a nice boy, but a bit *wild* – why, only the other day she saw him bicycling down the lane with his arms folded across his chest.

Well, before answering this specific question, one must know a good deal more about Willy. He may be an irrevocable risk-taker – there are a few – but more likely he needs a little discipline in the true sense of leadership by example, not the discipline of the cane. If he joins a good gliding club, this is exactly what he will get. When his fellow members, of all ages, see him show off or take an unnecessary risk, and unanimously call him, in the friendliest possible way, a silly clot for taking unnecessary risks with the club's property, and when he sees that the pilot most admired, and who probably is also the best pilot there, is the one who treats everything to do with flying with a careful and ordered respect, Willy may not only become a sound pilot, but at the same time possibly even a safer cyclist.

Of course any device which elevates the human frame into the air without visible means of support is potentially dangerous. But this is, surely, a challenge to be met by self-discipline and a careful, logical approach, and, tackled in such a way, the hazard is reduced to an acceptable minimum. There is one great difference between gliding and motoring – if you hurt yourself doing the former, it is extremely likely to be your own fault, whereas on the roads, the hazards of an accident occurring to you owing to the recklessness or carelessness of someone else are probably fifty per cent of the whole.

Let us look at it another way. Is motoring dangerous? It depends on whether you mean pleasure motoring or car-racing. Is shooting? Shooting what? Rabbits, or lions? Is gliding dangerous? Club gliding, ordinary sporting gliding, attempting height records in storm clouds, or competing for your country in World Championships?

The air is a stern disciplinarian. Handled carelessly, she exacts her punishments inexorably. The sailplane, being light and slow, and without any possibility of taking fire, does in the vast majority of cases limit the fine to one on the pocket only. But men have paid with their lives, and amongst them my greatest friend. The best we can do, and the most fitting, is to attempt from each such tragedy to draw the lesson of how to prevent its recurrence, so that the life lost may save future lives. To fail in this would be a tragedy and a betrayal.

* * *

The human beings who make up one man's – or woman's – world, are indeed few in number. He is a lucky man who needs the fingers of both hands on which to count them. And so what follows is, to me, a description of literally the most dreadful thing that has happened. And the only lesson from it is, that the High Alps are dangerous terrain – too dangerous – for world gliding contests, where the keenness to win honour for his country inevitably drives a man to attempt to beat the other fellow, regardless of normal standards of risk.

But this was the first post-war international meeting, and we had few standards, and no precedents, to go by. Ordinary pleasure and club gliding from Samaden, in the Engadine valley, had proved, and continues to be, quite safe, and no one realised the entirely different atmosphere of a highly competitive contest between the world's best pilots.

I shall fail to convey – I do not believe any writer could convey – the majesty and grandeur of the High Alps, seen from the bright cockleshell of a sailplane. Nor can I hope to communicate the instant, searing descent from exhilaration to a despair which will never entirely fade. But on this day, Kit Nicholson, Donald Greig and I lived and flew within a few yards and minutes of each other, through the same experiences and hopes and successes and failures, and saw the same unforgettable menaces and glories. I find I want – why do I want? – to make the attempt to show them to others. No one else can.

Gliding in the seventies: a Slingsby Kestrel 19 (*Daily Express*)

The problems of upcurrents and sink are more than ever present in mountain valleys.

15

THE DEAD END OF THE MALOJA WIND

The Maloja Wind is a strange and special meteorological phenomenon of the Engadine valley. In the morning, as the sun climbs, the hot and humid air of the Northern Italian plain is suddenly drawn up into the Alps through the gorge of Lake Como and the terrible defile of the Maloja Pass, where it is lifted over a mile in twelve miles, until it is pressed into the cold and clear length of the Engadine, the upper valley of the Inn, six thousand feet above sea-level, flanked by ten-thousand-foot mountains with transverse gorges gashing into each wall. It flows up the north-easterly course of this valley full of warmth and energy, bubbling up the side-valleys and mountain walls and rising in swift invisible columns, until it cools to form, at 14,000 feet, great flocculent piles of cumulus rivalling the white peaks of the mountains it has outclimbed. As the sun sets, this wind fades and dies, and by evening there is again a clear calm.

July 28th 1948 was the eighth day of the international gliding contests at Samaden. On this day three British sail-planes flew down the Maloja Pass to attempt the hitherto untried flight through the far source of the Maloja Wind and across the plains of north-western Italy. That evening the homing retrieving crews brought back only one.

At ten o'clock thirty sailplanes were stretched on the valley grass on each side of the starting line, quiet in the bright calm air. The mountains on both sides rose direct from the flat,

green floor of the valley into a sky of cloudless blue. At
10.15 a puff of wind stirred the windsock, and the scene
came to life. The Maloja Wind had started.

No. 17 was first off, climbed steeply to 1,000 feet on the
wire, released, and turned on to the neighbouring windward
slopes of Muottas Murail. Five minutes before the pine-
covered slope had been dead, now the attacking air had
brought it to life. No. 17 started to climb, tacking across and
across the mountainside in ascending lines. Other machines
quickly joined the erratic discipline. At 7,000 feet they outclimbed the tree-line and weaved up, only a span away from
the rock-face, to the level of the hotel on the crest, balanced
at the head of its funicular railway. Here No. 17 cut north-

24 *Samaden to Maloja Pass*

west across the flat floor of the valley to the 10,000-foot spine of Crasta Mora, and, seizing the powerful upwind, was soon a shadow in the underside of the cloud now capping the razor-back of the mountain.

He now turned south-west, on the course for Italy. At 11,000 feet he found lift and cloud over Piz Vair, and whilst he was circling in the ragged fringe over a snow-capped basin of mountain in and out of view beneath, his shadow circled into sight, out again, and then emerged close and clear in a bell-like dome in the base of the cloud. So close that he saw the white cap of his friend, so close that a wave of hands passed between them, Nos. 15 and 17 circled and climbed, moving images in a vast and lonely mirror. A puff

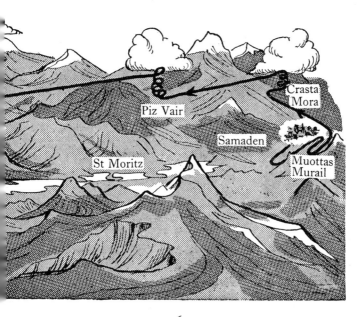

of vapour blurred between them, then as they lifted into cloud base, a momentary curtain. It was clearly unsafe to remain together. With one accord the two changed their courses and were lost between the white stalagmites of rock and stalactites of cloud. The mirror was empty again.

No. 17 once more set course south-west, and soon reached the head of the Maloja Pass. Quite suddenly here the mountains close in, and the road falls over the head of the valley,

25   *Maloja Pass to Como*

M. Berlin

Lago di Como

Dervio

zigzagging down a sheer precipice 1,000 feet high. As the sailplane entered this defile the air changed abruptly. It lost its life and sparkle and became gravid, misty and thick. Dead lumps of cloud hung on each wall, the sun broke through in unwilling patches, and lit only dimly the gorge beneath falling steeply away. No. 17 realised, too late, that the air had died. He could not find in it enough life to turn and climb back to the sunlit valley and mountains behind. He still had

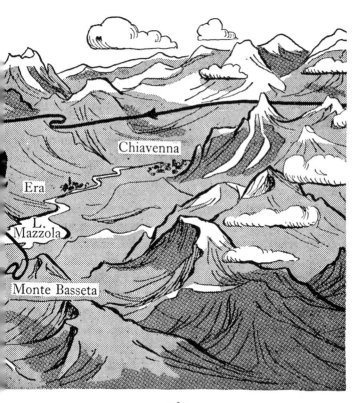

nearly 10,000 feet of height, not enough to clear the mountains on each side, but plenty to reach the wider reaches of the low Italian lakes, and although the air was nowhere rising, neither was it clawing him down. Turning and tacking round the chaotic lumps of cloud, he slid down, a quiet white shadow amidst the blacknesses of the Val Bregaglia, over the tiny villages hugging the tortured road. Vicosoprana and Castasegna drifted silently below; at Chiavenna the valley turned southward and widened, a flat plain opened, luxuriant with vineyards and maize fields, fading south into the haze but still prisoned on each side by mountains towering into cloud. But where gaps appeared in these clouds, they could be seen to rise into swelling Everests of cumulo-nimbus bulging up for miles out of the mists into clear, high air, dwarfing the hidden mountains. There was lift and life indeed, but unapproachable, because the base of each cloud was far down the mountain walls.

No. 17 was now about 3,000 feet above the valley floor, about 1,000 feet below the level of his take-off. He had nosed for lift into many of the cracks and crevices of the mountain wall and found little. The small Lago di Mazzola lay ahead, curving westward out of sight to the head of Lake Como itself, hidden by the intervening spine of Monte Bellinghera. A landing in the Piano di Chiavenna appeared possible, but a weak ending to his project. In the centre of the valley opposite the small village of Era, for the first time his instruments indicated a wide but feeble area of rising air. He circled delicately and again. For some fifteen minutes he circled, gaining perhaps 200 feet, and never saw it, never saw the taut and terrible violin-string, stretching from the westward mountain at an incredible height across to the opposite foot of the valley, the unmapped wire down which the mountaineers pulleyed their cut logs of wood to the valley markets.

He straightened his course and flew on along the western wall. At the westward curve he struck a violent down-draught and immediately realised the cause. The valley wind was sweeping up from Como and here the opposite, eastern, curve of the mountainside was deflecting it northward up to Maloja, whilst some was being turned over in a gigantic horizontal roll right across the valley to descend on the western side. Quickly, whilst he had the height, he crossed to where Monte Basseta formed a wedge separating the valley down which he had come from the tributary valley of Sondrio. Here was lift in abundance – the olive-trees on the mountainside were flattened by it.

Rising at 500 feet a minute, he tacked up, past a precipi-tous huddle of rough stone hovels where children stared and ran and waved, to 6,000 feet above the valley floor. Now he could take breath, he had a safe base from which to explore the next phase of his flight. He fished his packet of sand-wiches out from its crevice in the tiny cockpit, opened it, and started to eat. The time was 12.30.

Round the upper corner of the valley down which he had come, rather lower than he had been, crept the white shape of another machine. No. 18 had also descended the pass and entered the lower reaches. No. 17 never saw him, did not see the struggling shape reach the same weak lift near Era, did not see the first hesitant circle, the treachcrous delicate lift, the small white fragment that suddenly cut away from the port wing, the instant tilt and uplift of the undamaged wing, steep spiral dive into the mountain slope below, a puff and flurry of white splintered wood. After that there was nothing he could have seen, for Donald Greig had not jumped.

No. 17 finished his sandwiches. He saw the silver shape of his trailer crawl past on the road a mile below, heading south in search of him. He set off to explore the neighbourhood. He tried the southern wall of the Sondrio valley and found nothing. When he had lost half his height he returned again to Monte Basseta and climbed again to 6,000 feet. He now thrust out south-westward towards Lake Como and found a wide area of smooth and gentle lift that took him across to the head of the lake and on to the huge, south-facing amphitheatre of Monte Bellinghera.

Here the view broadened out and the full extent of the meteorological misfortune of the flight became evident. In drastic contrast to the clear and sparkling air of the upper valley, here only thirty miles away the whole deep, semi-tropical valley of Como seemed to steam up into sullen cloud. The wide violet waters of the lake were so directly contained by the mountains that even the lakeside road and railway were forced to flicker in and out of a series of tunnels. Grey shapeless lumps of cloud hung to the mountain sides, but still through the occasional rifts, in the far upper skies could be seen fantastic billows of cumulonimbus, thrusting perhaps six miles into the air.

To the south the haze thickened, and the far end of the lake, the way out of the nightmare into the plains, was blocked by the deep purple curtain of an advancing storm.

Monte Bellinghera formed a serrated spine across the northern end, and the dead and steamy wind was here thrust up until it formed a wide flat shelf of grey cloud, growing out of the mountainside at 6,000 feet like a gigantic tree-fungus. For some queer reason rags of cloud here and there formed far below on the flanks and ascended, growing as they came, until they were absorbed into this ceiling.

The spine of the mountain was deeply indented with a series of complicated ravines, into each of which No. 17 nosed for lift. Near the rocky walls gentle rise was to be found everywhere, blowing up into the sealing shelf of cloud.

At 2.15 p.m., a few minutes ahead of No. 17 and unseen by him, No. 15 had also turned into this complex of gulleys, flying just below the cloud. He entered a narrow V-shaped cleft and when he was near its apex suddenly he was enveloped by one of the ascending rags of cloud coming up from below. The air around him congealed, became opaque as the white of an egg instantly clouds when it is heated. He was blind, with mountain walls a few yards ahead, and to right and left of him. This was the vile trick which the air, instinct with the careless malignity of that valley and that day, played on No. 15 after his sixteen years' devotion to it.

He tried to turn out of the trap; the next moment the crags and boulders loomed up a few yards ahead. He pulled back hard, threw his aircraft's pitiful small reserve of energy into a desperate climb of perhaps a hundred feet, the wall of mountain disappeared, there was a dead, dead silence. The machine, all forward speed lost, dropped, struck and splayed. The wings, broken, stretched in their normal context across the line of the splintered fuselage. No. 15 lay, a shattered white cross, in thick cloud ten thousand feet up, amidst the huge boulders on the exact cruel spine of Monte Bellinghera.

Her pilot, conscious, called for help. A hundred feet below, but out of sight because of the cloud, No. 17 slid by, sucking a piece of barley sugar.

By an extraordinary chance the calls of the injured pilot were almost at once heard by a shepherd on the mountainside near by. The slow carriage down was started, but by nightfall it was only possible to reach an isolated chapel 3,000 feet above the valley, and here they found a Roman Catholic priest.

No. 17 continued on down the western wall of the lake, but soon the impossibility of his goal became evident. The whole valley seemed to offer only one chance of a landing. On the far eastern side was a patch of flat green, near the village of Dervio. At 2,000 feet he turned, crossed the lake; the green was a miraculous field, and he landed at 2.50 p.m. Thirty-five years before, an Englishman living at Dervio had wanted to play golf. The field was all that remained of his nostalgia, which had produced one fortunate result which he could not have foreseen.

When No. 17 reached the frontier with his retrieving crew that night, no news had yet been received of No. 18, but No. 15 was reported as having had both legs broken, and being on the way in an ambulance to the hospital at Chiavenna. It had started to rain as they turned and twisted back down the tortured road, and distant flashes of lightning occasionally and dramatically etched the serrated skyline crowding in so near on either side. At Chiavenna they turned into the narrow huddle of streets, directed by a native who had jumped on the bonnet of the car, undeterred by the warm rain. The hospital was a large sprawling stone building; in its wide corridors they were met by the serenity of a convent.

The nuns showed them to a surgery, where a French-speaking doctor and his assistants were waiting. Outside was the distant roar of the river, and the occasional rumble of the thunder. The doctor, stripped to his shirt-sleeves in the sullen heat, told them that the ambulance was expected in half an hour. Another car arrived bringing assistance from Samaden. The time dragged by, but at last the horn of an approaching car, feet outside; the doctor went out into the corridor. After a moment No. 17 followed ; the doctor was standing with a small group of newcomers. No. 17 asked urgently where was his friend. The doctor looked at him for a moment, then with a quiet, precise and final sympathy he said : 'Il est mort.'

The ambulance had returned empty. Insisting to the end that he would live and fly again, Kit Nicholson had dozed and died in the stone chapel on the mountainside. They brought him down the following day.

Fiction would not dare echo so wild and evil a coincidence, in which two fine and safe pilots were accidentally killed within two hours and two miles of each other from totally different causes. Yet this is a precise account, within the limits of known truth and acquired evidence, of the deaths of Donald Greig and Kit Nicholson.

Donald Greig – large, solid, reliable, a meticulous, painstaking and enthusiastic pilot.

Kit Nicholson – virile and sensitive, artistic yet intensely practical, brilliant architect, a man of a flashing gay courage and integrity, my dear friend.

16

BLIND FLYING IS A STATE OF MIND

I have left this special field of flying to be described last, because it is in many respects a separate and rather strange one, involving a new and additional set of techniques.

Few people realise how much of the brain's interpretation of sensations coming to it are modified by the information coming through the eyes. When sight is cut out, in darkness or cloud, and there are no outside visual references available to add to the signals coming from the other senses, the mind makes the most extraordinary mistakes of interpretation.

If you seat yourself on a revolving piano stool in absolute darkness, with your feet off the floor, and get someone to set it spinning, you will feel the *acceleration* as the stool gains speed, and hence interpret, correctly, that you have started to turn. Whilst you are spinning very rapidly, centrifugal force will throw the blood outward from the centre towards the surface of your body, and you will retain the sensation of turning. If the stool is fairly frictionless, however, so that it slows down very gradually, you will be unable to feel any sensation of slowing down, and you will be quite unable to report the moment when you stop turning.

Now imagine yourself seated in an aeroplane on a dark night. If the pilot does a loop, your body will report that it is accelerating *upwards*, owing to the sensation of being pushed upward by your seat. This sensation of upward acceleration will remain exactly the same during the second half of the loop, when you are in fact, *losing* height, because your seat is still pressing you 'upwards' towards the centre point of your loop: your body will transmit sensations which you interpret entirely wrongly.

If you are flying in a perfectly banked circle, the only physical sensation is again of being pushed upward by your seat, by virtue of the centrifugal force applied: again, in the absence of visual reference you will feel that you are climbing. You are in fact in both cases accelerating all the time towards the centre of your circle, and the fact that the circle is in one case vertical in relation to the earth, and in the other horizontal, can only be detected by the sight, and not, in its absence, by any of the other senses.

Reverting to the second half of the loop, when you feel as if you are climbing but are in fact diving, before very long other senses will start conflicting with your previous interpretation. As the aircraft gains speed in the dive, the noise of the air rushing past outside will increase, and accelerations of the blood in your head and elsewhere will produce feelings which, if unexpected, are unpleasant and may even be alarming.

When the mind loses confidence in its interpretations of the senses and doesn't know what to do next, vertigo and nausea step in, and the life of the pilot becomes quite complex.

The uninitiated may get a very exact idea of this difficulty by trying the old parlour joke with a walking-stick. Plant this on the floor, clasp the hands on the crook, then bend down and place the forehead on your hands, so that you are gazing at the floor. In this position shuffle five or six times round the stick, keeping its point stationary on the floor. Now stand upright, drop the stick, and walk in a straight

26   *Semi-circular canals*

line across the room. The sensations you feel whilst doing this are precisely those experienced by the beginner blind-flying pilot after doing a spin, or a number of circles, in his machine.

The pilot, however, is faced with the relatively more intricate task of controlling his machine in three dimensions, whilst his judgment is overshadowed by the rather nerve-racking possibilities which can arise from failure.

An understanding of the physical construction of the human mechanism of balance is useful to enable one to work out the kinds of misleading information which will come from it in any particular circumstances.

This mechanism, called the semi-circular canals, consists of three half-loops of hollow tube, filled with liquid, and situated in the skull near the inner organ of hearing. Each loop is in one of the three planes of direction. At around the mid-point of each loop, hair-like nerves stick out from one side, just failing to touch the other side (see above). On either side of the free ends of these nerves are small chalk lumps, bedded in the canal wall.

Any acceleration in the plane of the particular canal will tend to 'leave behind' the fluid inside, which will sweep the nerve-endings in that direction and cause them to be tickled by the knob to that side. This transmits a message to the brain: 'We are turning in my plane.'

If the turn continues steadily, friction between the canal walls and the contained fluid causes it to 'catch up', and the nerve-hairs return to their central position, reporting (wrongly): 'We are now going straight again.' When the body decelerates, and starts to come out of the turn, the fluid gets left behind again, in the opposite direction, carrying the nerve-hairs which report (wrongly again): 'We are now turning the other way.'

Putting this into tabular form, we get:

Attitude	*Sense interpretation*	
Straight flight	Straight flight	
Starting to turn	Starting to turn	
Continuing in steady turn	Straight flight again	
Coming out of turn	Starting to turn in opposite direction	
Remaining steady in straight flight	Straight flight	

This is no way to reach home!

It will be seen that, in the absence of sight, the semi-circular canals only give an impression of movement in any direction whilst the body is accelerating or decelerating – in fact, they interpret *the rate of change* of acceleration as acceleration, *rate of change* of movement (acceleration) as movement itself, and steady movement they interpret as rest.* When you are sitting in an aeroplane flying steadily at 300 m.p.h., if you shut your eyes, there is no sensation of movement at all.

To achieve controlled blind flight, therefore, a human being needs an instrument which is not so entirely unreliable – one which will continue to show 'turn' for as long as you are, in fact, turning. The basis of such an instrument lies in the properties of the gyroscope.

A spinning gyroscope resists very strongly any attempt to rotate it in a plane at right angles to its axis of rotation (or spindle), and if coupled in this plane to a needle registering on a dial, will register 'turn' through this needle until the turn is stopped. The basic instrument used for this purpose is the turn-and-bank indicator, which is sometimes, more properly, called the turn-and-slip indicator.

But to provide an instrument of this kind is not enough: the pilot has to discipline his mind in its use. At first when, flying in cloud, one's senses start conveying misleading sensations to the brain which conflict with the indications of the turn-and-bank indicator, the conditioned reflexes built up over many years are likely to be too strong for the

---

* Mathematically expressed, their error is to show:
$$\frac{d^2v}{dt^2} = \frac{dv}{dt} \; ; \; \frac{dv}{dt} = v \; ; \; v = 0$$

reasoning powers, and instinctively the feet and hands make the control movements dictated by the information coming from the senses. It is rather like one's early struggles at learning to ride a bicycle, but considerably complicated by being in three dimensions and a much more unnatural environment.

In the early stages, very powerful and exhausting efforts of will are required to force oneself to ignore one's senses and obey instead the dictates of the instrument; and the indications of the two needles, not being at all similar to the indications received through the eyes when they are working, involve inferential interpretation which adds greatly to the mental labour required.

Gradually, with practice, the pilot's instrumental interpretation becomes more automatic. His first efforts, which may produce mental exhaustion and surrender in a minute or less, lead to slowly greater endurance times.

Eventually, however, the senses are overcome, or at least repressed, and the sailplane pilot reaches a stage where he can 'switch on' a special state of mind in which he cuts out his sensual feelings and automatically responds to his instruments instead. There used to be a body of opinion holding that, even when this stage has been reached, there tends to be a kind of secondary exhaustion period every twenty minutes or so, but from my own experience I am inclined to think that this is not so, or at any rate does not apply to everyone : certainly I do not now notice it in myself.

It is important and interesting to note that in this matter the pure sailplane pilot may have a special claim to expertise beyond that of the aeroplane pilot. The reason is that aeroplanes, with their extra size, weight, cost and load-carrying capacities, are equipped with additional and more complex blind-flying instruments which present to the pilot a more natural picture of the true attitude of his machine in space, and so enormously reduce the possible mental fatigue of blind flying. Thus the modern aeroplane pilot does not have to achieve anything like the degree of skill in flying on the simple turn-and-bank indicator as does the sailplane pilot: indeed, in most blind flying the aeroplane flies through cloud on a straight course on its automatic pilot, with its human pilot more or less unemployed. In contrast to this, the sailplane pilot is for most of the time flying in unstable cloud, and doing complicated manœuvres in order to keep in the lift, of the type most likely to produce vertigo.

When, however, the aeroplane pilot does, for any reason, assume direct control of his craft, he has, in addition to the turn-and-bank indicator, an instrument called the Artificial Horizon to assist him. This instrument consists, broadly, of a circular black face, across the centre of which is scribed a straight horizontal white line, which is simply interpreted as the natural horizon. In front of this white line is suspended the outline of a model aeroplane, and in normal level flight the wings of this are directly superimposed on the horizon-line. In a bank, the line banks in relation to this model, exactly as the invisible horizon banks in relation to the wings of the aircraft itself; and in a climb or dive the artificial horizon-line rises or sinks above or below the model.

Thus the pilot's eyes see a model of what is actually happening to his aeroplane in space, and no inferences have to be drawn by his brain: accordingly no excessive expenditure of mental energy is called for.

It is interesting also to record that, when aeroplane pilots with experience of the artificial horizon take to gliding, they usually find it desirable to fit an artificial horizon to their sailplanes, to achieve a satisfactorily accurate standard of manœuvring in cloud, in spite of the extra weight, complication and expense involved. *Ab initio* sailplane pilots, however, who have never experienced such soft living, can frequently achieve equally good results on the turn-and-bank indicator alone.

The artificial horizon, in exaggerated aircraft attitudes, can 'topple', and cease to register, whereas the turn-and-bank indicator continues functioning in all circumstances. It is accordingly a more fundamentally reliable instrument, though not so easy to learn to use for long periods.

There is thus, to my mind, quite a possibility that, as high-performance gliding instruction becomes more easily available, probably through the medium of high-performance two-seater sailplanes, it will have a direct application in one aspect of the training of both civil and military aeroplane pilots.

On Sunday, 5th June 1938, I took off from the site of the London Gliding Club, on Dunstable Downs, in my Minimoa. The time was 3 p.m. The conditions were good, but not extremely so, and I had no idea of going for a height record. At about 4.30, however, I struck a strong upcurrent, and in company with a friend in another machine circled rapidly up to the base of a small cloud over Luton, at about 4,500 feet. From here I could see a rather large storm cloud building up over Leighton Buzzard, some eight miles to the west, so flew towards this.

As I got nearer it became clear that there was a very active current of air ascending into it. The base looked quite flat, as is the case with nearly all active cumulus clouds, except that along the far edge there seemed to be a darker slate-grey area

– denoting a greater depth of cloud-vapour above – bordered by a hanging ragged fringe which could be seen to form constantly and to be constantly ascending into the cloud above. As I approached this my rate-of-climb indicator showed increasing lift, until it moved up to a climb of 10 feet per second. I put the machine into a circle and spiralled rapidly upwards.

At this point the rapid upcurrent of air had lifted the apparently flat ceiling of cloud somewhat, so that I spiralled up into a kind of diving bell, the walls formed of blue-grey cloud, with below a reducing circle of sunlit green fields. The base of this bell sank slowly down, we approached the ceiling, and everything vanished. The time I went into the cloud was 5.10 p.m., the height about 4,900 feet.

Entering a big cloud in a sailplane is a very different experience from doing the same thing in an aeroplane, for in the powered craft the general noise and vibration over-shadow the subtler flavours of flight. I had a feeling that we had been absorbed by a large and immensely powerful octopus. The rush of air over the wings took on a different key and became smoother and quieter: one felt as though entrapped within an envelope of almost sticky power. The hue of the surrounding vapour, a bluish black, was octopus-like also. This of course was due to the great thickness of the cloud at this point, for I subsequently discovered it was more than a mile high. It is only the shallower clouds or the fringes of the big ones which assume the more friendly tones of white or light grey.

The rate of climb now gradually increased to 15 feet a second, the only sound being the comforting buzz of the little electric motor of my turn indicator. For a while the air rose smoothly and swiftly, then we struck a rough area, and the machine started to lurch. Simultaneously, I began to feel marked vertigo, my head started to swim, and my senses to convey impressions quite different from those recorded by my instruments.

Before going into the cloud I had marked that the edge nearest to my point of entry lay to the north, so I now straightened the machine from its right-handed circles (which operation gave me the most violent, but false, impression of doing a steep left-hand climbing turn), and held her rather grimly on a northerly compass course, which about five minutes later brought us out of a towering wall of dazzling cloud into the sunlight at 7,500 feet.

I flew around, losing height, for a few minutes until the vertigo had subsided, then headed back into the cloud. My intention was to fly straight through it and out on the other side, but after negotiating a very violent downcurrent which shot me down at nearly 20 feet a second, I struck a smooth patch of air rising nearly as fast, so again put my machine into a circle and climbed very fast indeed.

Now ice started to form on all protuberances, on the front of the cockpit cover and the leading edge of the wings. However, I did not meet any rain or hail, which is usual in such clouds, and I knew that Minimoas had emerged successfully from much more severe conditions after cloud flights in Germany, so was not worried on that score. But the nervous strain is considerable for the amateur, and it was with some relief that I saw the needle of my altimeter at last top 10,000 feet, which was the height I had set myself to reach. I straightened up again and steered a southerly course. The surrounding cloud gradually lightened, then a gap appeared ahead. With joy I anticipated seeing the earth again, and the long quiet glide down and back to tea at the club-house.

But I was disappointed. I came out of my cloud to find, far beneath me, apparently stretching in all directions, the bulging tops of an unbroken sea of cumulus. Behind me, a mountain of white rising out of the white plain beneath, my storm cloud towered yet another 1,500 feet up into the blue sky. It was a sight to dazzle the gods, but to me it was a pain in the neck. I wanted tea, not ambrosia.

It was 5.45. I had been thirty-five minutes inside the cloud. As I slowly descended towards the cloud-sheet beneath I searched for a gap through which I might descend without having to do further blind flying, with the possibility of encountering more unwanted lift inside the clouds; at length I did in fact find a small gap through which I could see, an incredible distance below, a vista of green and brown fields and a road. I circled steeply down through this, occasionally penetrating the surrounding clouds, and emerged a short while later just to the north of Luton, my cloud having drifted about eight miles whilst I was inside it.

I set the nose of Minimoa back west for Dunstable and had a good look round. Along the leading edge of the wings, 58 feet in span, ran a three-quarter inch ribbon of jagged ice crystals, having exactly the same appearance as one of those rubber nail-brushes. Similar crystals had formed in front of my transparent cockpit-cover and on various protuberances on the outside of the machine. In absolute silence we planed down to 4,000 feet, when a sharp crack made me jump in my seat. I looked anxiously around. Then a spark of watery light flew by, and a lump of ice, melted from the nose, flew back and hit the wing with a crack like splintering wood. Next, similar sounds started from the tail, and it was quite a relief when, at about 2,000 feet, the last white fragments had gone and all was again quiet.

The landing was at 6.15, and the height recorded on my barographs was subsequently officially confirmed at 10,080 feet, which established a new British height record.

Apart from an isolated adventure, prior to 1936 there had been no proper attack by British sailplane pilots on the problems associated with blind flying in unstable cloud.

There were at that time possibly a few who thought they had been born blind flyers, there were many who were to achieve blind flying, but now there came some who had blind flying thrust upon them; the consequences were in some cases considerably more drastic than we had anticipated.

In Hjordis I had at last achieved a machine equipped for blind flying, and so started rather nervously nibbling at clouds. I employed the technique of circling into a cloud as nearly as possible to one edge, so that when and if I had had enough I could come out in quite a short time by straightening up and steering a compass course for the adjacent edge. I found that in any turbulence the best I could do was from five to ten minutes, after which one's mental resistance seems to become exhausted. In smooth cloud however it is easier, and on one occasion I circled quite happily for perhaps fifteen minutes and nearly 2,000 feet until I decided to come out on account of heavy snow.

This experience no doubt produced over-confidence, so that on June 7th, at Bradwell Edge after a rather abortive week's holiday, failing to soar in bitter north-east winds and rain, I circled into a rather amorphous and large mass of grey cloud at about 2,500 feet without locating an adjacent edge or anything else.

It was mildly, but not excessively, turbulent inside; the lift also was only mild, from 2 feet to 7 feet a second, and in a gay and youthful spirit I straightened up once or twice and went searching for better patches, in which I started circling and manœuvring again.

Suddenly the instruments went completely wild. I worked out afterwards that I must have stalled: the nose drops, speed builds up; one corrects, but there is a lag in the registering of the air-speed indicator, so one stalls again, more violently; the nose drops a second time, speed goes up higher; a third stall was followed by Bedlam.

The turn indicator jammed hard left, the bank indicator hard right. The variometer showed its maximum of 25 ft./sec. descent, but as we were certainly losing height at over 150 ft./sec. maybe it had gone round six times. The air-speed indicator however exercised in me the greatest and most baleful fascination. It was registering a seemingly innocuous 40 m.p.h., but I had watched it with popping eyes achieve this by going twice round the dial. Hjordis, feeling as tight as a drum, was bellowing like a bull in pain, and perhaps the most dominant of my kaleidoscopic emotions was a fixed desire to move nothing more than an inch at a time.

It can be imagined that few actual seconds of this elapsed before I burst out of cloud-base in a dive rather over the vertical, and in full view of those on the ground. From this I gradually extracted her, and with the last of my excess speed I zoomed back into the base of the cloud. There was at that moment no spot in three-dimensional space which I would not have preferred; fortunately the maw failed at this time to clutch, and shortly afterwards we got clear.

The heroes of this story are (a) Buxton, designer of Hjordis, and (b) Slingsby, her constructor. I fill the role of foolish virgin. For, spurred on by this experience, I started, rather late in the day, to read up the subject.

I discovered that the entertainment sprung on me was the High Speed Spiral Dive, which I now give respectful capitals, and that it is a standard experience for any who attempt blind flying without proper instruction.

Part of the difficulty in obtaining accurate information regarding the difficulties of blind flight lies in many pilots' fear that an admission that they have been in trouble will imply lack of skill. Many pilots have on occasion flown for considerable periods without blind-flying instruments in smooth cloud without getting into trouble, though they will probably admit that on those occasions the machine has really been left to fly itself.

In fact, even birds are unable to fly blind; pigeons have been blindfolded and released from aeroplanes, and in every case have proved helpless, doing spins and spiral dives.

This may sound like an attempt to put people off; in fact, however, the thing appears to be to abolish the pilot's erroneous confidence in his senses, and then build up an *instinctive* confidence in his instruments. *Blind flying is a state of mind.*

The moral of all this will no doubt be drawn by everyone for himself, according to his own taste. Some will say (some do say) that the moral is 'Don't'. Yet the subject has enormous possibilities for enhanced technique and the enjoyment of new fields of beauty.

What *is* definitely wrong is to go on happily flying into clouds and mist without adequate equipment and without full knowledge of what is involved. For the deductions are:

(1) That no machine is strong enough to stand up to what *may* be inflicted on it in clouds. The chances of break-up are small, but the *risk* is unavoidable. (Moral: parachute.)

(2) That no pilot born of woman can fly blind for long without instruments, although one may get away with it the first few times. (Moral: instruments.)

(3) That the successful use of blind-flying instruments is a difficult art. (Moral: lessons.)

When, however, someone comes down and airily confesses to having flown the club's ten-year-old moth-eaten Wobling intentionally into a cloud, he should at once be sent off to choose his site in the local cemetery. I think most pilots will agree that the reaction to this cloud-flying business must be: 'Go ahead, but first realise fully *what it involves*, and take the necessary precautions.'

It is my firm opinion, irrespective of what better men than I may have said elsewhere, that really serious sailplane blind flying cannot be safely self-taught. No one should venture into a big cloud in a sailplane until he has been given dual in spin recovery under a hood, and if possible (though this is harder to come by) in recovery from high-speed spiral dives.

Blind flying is perfectly easy *until things go wrong*, when in the twinkling of an eye it becomes very difficult indeed unless one's instincts have been got under control by previous practice. And one cannot give oneself practice in spins and spiral dives, or in any way known to me force oneself through the necessary but unpleasant process of learning to keep control of one's steed, whilst subject to the nauseating and misleading sensations of vertigo. I may say that, for me, the Link trainer produced no symptoms, and a genuine aircraft was essential.

Ten years had passed since the events of the last section, of which six had been spent occupied in more serious, if less fascinating, pursuits than sporting gliding.

Time and events had brought the business of blind flying into focus, and the happy-go-lucky approach of those early days had given way to a sound and sensible attitude.

On 19th June 1946 I flew my Weihe from the Long Mynd, near Shrewsbury, to Molesworth, near Cambridge. The wind was light and west-north-west, almost straight up the hill. The forecast talked of cumulus, showers, occasional thunder and such-like intoxicating delights, but a slight shadow was cast by talk of a small Polar Low over Bristol travelling south-east and then east.

However, I decided to declare Cambridge as a goal, and also it was an obvious day to go for altitude on the way. I took off at 11.30; the wind was just strong enough for a bunjie launch and a very gentle climb up to 400 feet. Then, just north of the club-house, I struck lift up to 10 feet a second, and twelve minutes after take-off was at cloud-base, 2,000 feet above take-off altitude and half-way back to Church Stretton. I switched on the turn-and-bank indicator, and hardly switched it off again for three hours.

I circled up in fairly gentle lift in this first cloud to 3,000 feet (I will talk in general in altitudes above take-off. To get altitude above sea-level add the height of the Mynd, about 1,350 feet, throughout), and then set off on my course, approximately 105° magnetic, still in cloud.

The main difficulty of the day was that the clouds were in large untidy lumps all over the place, and rather widely spaced apart, and cloud-base was only just over 3,000 feet above sea-level, a scandalous state of affairs in midsummer weather. Thus it was necessary to keep above cloud-base as much as possible, and this I achieved, being above this level and in cloud for three hours out of the four and a quarter hours of the flight. But in this condition one hardly ever got a good view of the clouds around; when one came out for a few minutes, ragged and titanic masses of tumbled cloud were all round, and one could not see the wood for the trees.

It was also necessary on these brief occasions to locate oneself from the glimpse of the shadowed world through the hole beneath, but fortunately my war time A.T.A. past stood me in good stead, as in the last few years, ferrying aircraft, I had come to know England from above in a pretty comprehensive way.

I came out of my first cloud over the southern end of Wenlock Edge, and almost immediately entered another just ahead, from which rain was falling fairly heavily. The lift was ahead of the rain, which I first flew through, and circled up rather slowly to 3,500 feet. Here, to my dismay, my small German turn-and-bank stopped working, and when from the complaining noises from the Weihe I realised this, I clapped on the airbrakes and let her sort herself out whilst I fiddled with the $4\frac{1}{2}$-volt torch battery in its container, eventually to my relief finding a faulty contact and getting the instrument going again.

I had lost about 600 feet doing this, but on putting off the dive-brakes I found I was still in lift, and started circling again.

At 6,000 feet we started to ice up, ice building up forward of all protuberances and on the leading edge of the wing. The pressure head of the pitot tube grew its ice-straw, just as in the old days, the war seeming to have made little difference to the habits of cumulo-nimbus; and the rubber nail-brush of ice sprouted forward of the wing.

At 7,000 feet we reached rough air and the apparent top of the local lift, so went on again. As we came down, the airspeed indicator started to flicker and die as the ice-straw started to melt, so I kept straight on the turn-and-bank and let the Weihe fly herself until at 4,500 feet the lump of ice melted enough to blow off, struck the wind-screen with a resounding crack and disappeared, leaving me with a registering air-speed, which exchange I much preferred.

I fiddled about for some time in rather unsatisfactory lumps of medium-sized cumulus, never high enough to be really at ease, until I worked my way as far as Honiley, when I saw to the north towards Elmdon (Birmingham) a towering mass of cloud towards which I flew.

Gaining in cunning, I did not start circling at the first piece of lift, which I found near its edge, as I had come to the conclusion that this only took one up into the edges of the main mass of the cloud, but flew on through this and a few downcurrents, until I calculated that I was nearer the real bulk overhead. I then started circling in lift that gradually built up to 15 feet a second.

At 6,000 feet we re-assumed our excrescences of ice, and at 8,000 feet a fine powder of snow started to penetrate crevices of the cockpit cover. At 8,300 feet I started to get out of the cone of lift, probably through faulty circling, and as I was by now shivering with cold, I straightened once more on my course and set off in a glide at 50 miles an hour.

Back below 6,000 feet the air-speed indicator again faltered and went out, and now I was faced with quite a problem. If I encountered big lift again before I got low enough to recover my A.S.I., I was in no condition to meet it. However, it was a bridge which did not have to be crossed, because I came down, lost my ice-lump at 4,500 feet, and emerged for a brief four minutes at 3,600 feet, just in time to locate myself as north of Coventry, before flying once more into the side of another large cloud-mass.

Soon I struck big stuff. The green ball went up to 15, 20, 25 feet a second, and then disappeared into the top of the tube. I passed again through the icing level, then the powdery snow brought on the shivers again. This time it came in in quantities and covered the inside of the cockpit, and I had to wipe it off the face of the instruments. It also covered a good deal of me, got into my shoes, and in general I must have looked like a modern, if rather cramped, edition of Father Christmas.

I started to suck a toffee, a trick which I find rather consoling in these moments, and suddenly bit on a hard lump, which investigation showed to be a bit of tooth. Over the constricted panorama of my rather ascetic little world was superimposed a vision of my dentist's waiting-room which sports a particularly opulent line of large electric fire. This vision of my earthly life was rather comforting.

At 11,000 feet (12,350 feet above sea-level) I again met turbulent air, and having no clues about the sort of shape of the cloud I was in, could do no more than once again set sail for Cambridge. Once more through the reverse sequence, blocked A.S.I. and all, for over half an hour I sailed along through grey and lifeless cloud, until I came out and found myself almost on course near Kettering.

Ahead the cumulus did not look very hopeful, but I struggled on until, south of Thrapstone, I came to the very last cumulus, and found the remaining twenty-five miles ahead absolutely dead. Evidently Bristol's Polar Low had foiled me.

At least four airfields were in sight, so I picked the one that showed most signs of occupation, approached it at 110 m.p.h., and landed at 15.45 hours at Molesworth, 25 miles short of my goal.

17

BIG STUFF

The reader will realise that surprising and even violent things happen inside cumulo-nimbus clouds: it is not long since aeroplane pilots were told to avoid them at all costs, because of the horrid mysteries inside.

But such bogies can best be tackled by actually learning what does go on, and why, and this is what sailplane pilots have been doing over the last fifteen years. Although a great number of these clouds occur in conditions which make them unapproachable, over mountains or in the midst of cold frontal masses, sailplane flights in cumulo-nimbus are now fairly frequent, and if approached with the necessary knowledge, skill and caution, reasonably safe.

A cumulo-nimbus cloud is formed by the release of latent heat when an upcurrent reaches condensation-level on a day when the lapse rate is greater than the adiabatic lapse rate for saturated air (see page 43). In suitable conditions, the energy released is gigantic, and these clouds can reach up to over 40,000 feet.

Figure 27 shows a cross-section of a typical cloud. As the saturated air accelerates upwards, raindrops are formed and commence to fall. The terminal velocity of a raindrop, however, is about 27 feet per second. If the rain falls into a region of the cloud where the air is ascending faster than this, each drop will become suspended in the upcurrent and start to grow larger by collection of other drops. When it reaches

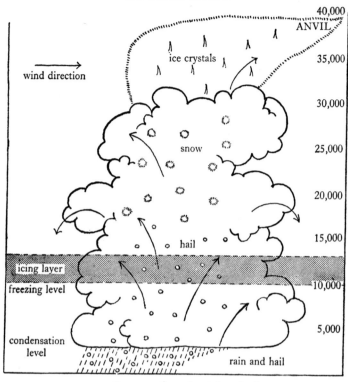

27   *Structure of cumulo-nimbus cloud*

a size of about 5 millimetres, the drop will be split up and the water carried up again in a fine spray, highly charged electrically. In this way the upper region of the cloud will become charged with an enormous electric potential, which may eventually discharge in the form of lightning. Lightning therefore, and its consequence, thunder, is a sure sign of up-currents in excess of 27 feet per second, or about 20 m.p.h.

If the condensation takes place above freezing level, small hailstones may be formed, and fall through the cloud. These attract a coating of moisture when they get below freezing level, and if they too fall into a region of the cloud where the upcurrent is strong enough, they also get carried up again. When above the freezing level again, this layer of moisture freezes on to the original stone, which thereby becomes larger and heavier, and will therefore fall faster. However, it may again be carried up, and repeat the cycle many times, each time getting larger and heavier. Eventually the stones will reach a size large enough to batter their way down through the upcurrent and fall to the ground.

Thus the size of a hailstone reaching the ground forms a basis for a fairly accurate calculation of the strength of up-current in the cloud above which was necessary for its for-mation, and stones the size of golf-balls, or larger, sometimes met in countries such as South Africa, require upcurrents of the order of 200 m.p.h. for their formation.

If a hailstone is cut in half, the cross-section will be seen to consist of concentric rings of ice, like the rings of a sawn tree-trunk; each ring indicating one up-and-down journey inside the cloud.*

In England, upcurrents of 40 feet per second or, say, 30 m.p.h., are about the strongest we have so far met, and so long as the flying speed of the sailplane is held to a reasonable figure the impact of the hail so formed is not dangerous, although the noise of its hammering on the wings and fuse-lage of a silent aircraft is quite impressive.

After climbing through the darkness, the drumming rain, the icing layer, and the roar of hail, the pilot reaches a quiet

* This theory of hail-formation shows signs of being supplanted by another which I will not attempt to describe. It may require modifica-tion of the 200-m.p.h. updraught figure, perhaps bringing it down to a niggardly 100 m.p.h. From the pilot's point of view, either figure is too much.

region of fine snowflakes and cold, dark cloud, gradually lightening as he approaches nearer the summit. As the sailplane reaches the upper portion and becomes highly charged with static electricity, some sparking may take place between metal parts and possibly the pilot, though most such parts are bonded. This may prick, but does not seem to be more than slightly tiresome.

It is essential, however, to seal all holes and cracks in the cockpit, to preserve the pilot from icy water and snow, and enable him to keep reasonably warm.

When he at last emerges from this rather odd pleasure, probably through the very rough eddies near the edges of the cloud, the scene which suddenly and dramatically spreads before his eyes is of a literally incomparable order of size and grandeur. This is another of the unforgettable experiences reserved only for the sailplane pilot.

June the 23rd 1946 marked the zenith of a week's remarkable flying by the Cambridge University Gliding Club during the first organised post-war camp held at the Long Mynd in Shropshire, the site of the Midland Club.

After some 400 hours' soaring, this particular flight from beginning to end was entirely unlike any other that I had ever experienced. The weather broadcast said that a high-pressure area to the south-west of Ireland had developed a ridge running north-east as far as south-east Scotland. The forecast was fine and warm, with some showers and possible thunderstorms on the north-west coast and North Wales, but no one seemed to anticipate that the air was going to achieve well-nigh explosive instability over a wide area.

In Church Stretton, in the valley nearly 1,000 feet below and to the east of the Mynd, there was a morning ground fog, though on the heather moor of the Mynd itself it was clear, with a view to the west over the top of the mist clamped down in Asterton valley. The surface wind was light and variable, and on the whole drifting down the hill from north-east, whilst the upper wind was light and northerly.

At 11.30 Pringle was winched in the Blue Gull, and came down to report only very slight occasional lift of the order of half a foot a second under the cloud-base at 600 feet.

At 12.00 I was launched in the Weihe. I had declared Cardiff airport, 65 miles to the south, as a goal, one reason being that from the forecast I believed that instability would be greatest in the western, coastal districts of England and Wales, and from the cumulo-nimbus already visible to the west and north-west it was clear that an altitude flight was a possibility.

The chances were that my flight would only become a delayed descent of perhaps 10 minutes after the launch, so considerable optimism was required to don warm boots, flying overalls, mark out my maps, prepare my barographs, put a pair of pyjamas and spongebag in the back locker and make the other preparations required for an advanced flight.

When I took off, cloud-base was about 700 feet above the Mynd, the cumuli were flat and ill-defined and clearly in a very early stage of growth. Nevertheless, on releasing at only 400 feet, I turned under one of these cloudlets and found lift of the order of 1 to 2 feet a second. By careful manœuvring I worked up to 700 feet, and then for over an hour found myself committed to an astonishing game of a sort of tiny tot's blind flying display. Directly over the club site, almost in earshot of the criticisms of those on the ground, I circled and manœuvred in and out of the low, ragged puffs of cloud and in spite of the down-hill drift and the low altitude, found broken lift in every one. The best lift seemed to be at the edges, half in and half out of the cloud, though hardly one complete circle showed rise all the way round. Thus in the rough air I frequently disappeared into a cloud at a stately 40 miles an hour, got tipped up on the inside half of the circle by a downcurrent, and whistled out a few seconds later at an undignified 55 miles an hour, no doubt to the jeers of the spectators beneath. However, as time went on, it was clear that the clouds over the Mynd were gradually building up, and slowly my efforts produced on balance an increase in altitude.

On my clear-air half circles an astonishing and unusual cloudscape became visible. My own clouds were, as I have said, based at only about 700 feet over the Mynd, which is itself about 1,350 feet above sea-level, but over the valley, just to the east, the early morning mist had lifted and was forming small cumuli based below the surface Mynd level, whilst the tops of these cumuli were only about the same height as the bottom of the Mynd ones.

When on the other hand one circled out into clear air on the western side of the Mynd, large cumulo-nimbus clouds could be seen to west and north-west, already obviously strong and towering up to around 15,000 feet. One particularly strong one had come into sight to the west-south-west about 15 miles away, and appeared to be coming cross-wind towards us.

I understand that the cloud which was developing over the Mynd, and in which I was circling, is a standard phenomenon there in light wind thermal conditions, and as it developed I slowly climbed until I had reached a height of around 5,000 feet in a cloud like an extraordinarily narrow twisted pillar of smoke nearly a mile high. I then estimated that from this height I could reach the cumulo-nimbus to the west-south-west which I had already marked down, and set off for it.

I flew for about 15 minutes in dead calm air, well over the tops of the small cumuli which by now dotted the sky in every direction, and as I got nearer I saw that my cloud had indeed developed into a giant, far bigger than the ones I had had experience of the week before. As I got nearer it obscured the whole of the south-western sky, heavy rain was falling from one sector, and overhead a huge anvil stretched out as a canopy.

I reached the fringes of the lower part at 2,000 feet (above take-off), and immediately the air became turbulent. As I went on I encountered lift and started to circle. I entered the cloud at 3,000 feet and climbed not very fast until when I seemed to have got as high as I could I turned, still in cloud, on to a west-south-west compass course to get farther into the heart of the storm.

I struck more lift, circled again, and again when I seemed to have got as high as possible turned west-south-west. Soon I struck strong lift, and some heavy raindrops cracked against the cockpit cover. From now on I became too busy to store up very detailed recollections, so much happened in so short a time.

The green ball of the rate-of-climb indicator disappeared into the top of its tube, and the rain got heavier and heavier, drumming on the fuselage and starting to bubble through cracks in the cockpit lid. Unlike on previous similar climbs, I did not on this occasion experience the forward building up of icicles on all excrescences including the pitot tubes, which usually means the loss of one's air-speed indicator when it melts on the way down. Freezing level was about 10,000 feet (above take-off) and although the cockpit cover was quickly obscured by ice my view outside was sufficiently featureless anyway for me not to miss it, being confined to a few feet of wing disappearing into the murk.

To me the remarkable flavour of these flights is given by the tiny size to which one's world contracts. The view comes down to a curved sheet of celluloid obscured by ice-crystals an inch or so to each side and above one's head, and a small panel of instruments dancing about two feet in front by one's knees. The cloud outside is a blind engine of some millions of horsepower, and it is not difficult to start imagining that it dislikes one.

Meanwhile, the large needle of the altimeter was going round nearly twice as fast as the second hand of a watch, and in one minute I rose over 2,000 feet. Such a rate of climb without powered assistance is difficult to visualise. If I had jumped overboard and pulled the rip-cord of my parachute, I should merely have reduced my rate of ascent by less than a half.

The air was more turbulent than usual in these violent upcurrents and the Weihe, in spite of its wonderful handling qualities, was thrown about, the speed varying between 35 and 60 miles an hour as we rocketed round. Each time the speed got too high for comfort, I straightened up on the turn-and-bank needles and eased it off on the elevator, then went again into the turn. The variation in the scream of the air as the speeds altered, and the crackling roar of rain and then hail on the machine provided a somewhat awe-inspiring background, and in addition to watching my instruments I soon had to be watching myself for signs of oxygen lack as, adding the 1,350 feet or so of the take-off altitude to my own, I was reaching a height above sea-level where this begins to affect judgment.

However, I immediately found, what every invalid knows, that if one is watching oneself for ailments, one immediately detects undoubted symptoms of every known disease from cholera to housemaid's knee, and the upshot was that when my altimeter showed I was approaching 17,000 feet above sea-level, with no least sign of a lessening ferocity of the upcurrent, I decided to straighten up and fly out of the storm. I found some little difficulty in doing this; several times I got the machine on an even keel for a split second when a violent gust threw one wing up and put me into a turn again. However, by working away I eventually got on to a south-easterly course, which would bring me out of the storm in the direction of my goal at Cardiff and about a quarter of an hour later emerged into a sunlit but rather awe-inspiring world.

The left-hand half was peaceful enough. Far below the fields and hills of Hereford and Gloucestershire were visible through numberless white puffs of cumulus woolpacks, the tops of which were still some two miles below me. But the whole of the right-hand half and the sky immediately above me was obscured by the storm cloud, which seemed to stretch as far as I could see over Central Wales.

The 'anvil' of the storm cloud, that huge characteristic shelf which forms at the top of the downwind side of a really big cumulo-nimbus, formed an immense grey canopy overhead, so that I was flying in a kind of half tunnel, sun, blue sky, white clouds and green fields to my left, grey cloud overhead, and every colour from grey to indigo-black to the right, where a curtain of cloud five miles high dropped from the anvil and clamped down on the dimly-seen craggy mountains of Wales, which disappeared into smoky screens of torrential rain, split every now and then by flashes of lightning.

At nearly 17,000 feet, I did not appear to be much more than half-way up this giant curtain!

I had no least doubt that the world's sailplane altitude record was waiting to be broken in that stuff; the upcurrents must have gone to heights of the order of 30,000 feet, but I had still less doubt in deciding to leave it unbroken. I later heard that all over the country cloudbursts of extraordinary violence had occurred and on the Mynd one washed away the road up from Church Stretton. I was getting a front-row view of an unusually violent weather phenomenon.

I was too high to locate myself, but flew on a compass course in silent smooth air for three-quarters of an hour, by which time I was down to 7,000 feet, but to my right was still the wall of the storm, stretching into the far distance. I now found I was approaching a region of still smoky air where for some extraordinary reason there were clearly no upcurrents, and it therefore appeared that after all I was going to be denied my goal flight to Cardiff.

After a great deal more hard work such indeed proved to be the case. I located myself at Ross-on-Wye, worked up in a cumulus to 7,000 feet, and set off in an attempt to reach Cardiff from this in a straight glide. I failed to find another ripple in the sky and landed after five hours in the air at Newport, eight miles short of my goal.

The greatest altitude reached was of the order of 17,000 feet above sea-level, but for record purposes the height of the launching-point and the height attained on the launch before release has to be subtracted. The height was 15,247 feet, a new British record.

Lastly, the lessons to be drawn. I suggest that from the sail-flying point of view a distinction seems necessary between major and minor cumulo-nimbus. I think the visual difference may well be that a major one has an anvil, and a minor one has not. By and large the minor one probably runs up to about 17,000 feet (the word 'minor' being relative only), and the major one to over 35,000 feet. The former should be treated with the utmost respect, the latter with a degree of awe.

The last flight will indicate two further problems which we now had to overcome: icing and oxygen.

Why, and when, does ice accrete on an aircraft? The answer lies in another extraordinary trick of the air. Water turns into ice at freezing-point, or 0° Centigrade, which sounds obvious enough. But cloud droplets have the remarkable property of being able to remain in the liquid state, if undisturbed, between temperatures of zero and minus ten degrees Centigrade; they can even sometimes remain liquid down to as low as −40° C. But if such 'supercooled' water droplets are suddenly agitated, they instantly congeal into tiny ice-crystals, and if the source of agitation is a rapidly moving solid object, such as the wing of an aircraft, they adhere to it. Even more complicated is the fact that they can form on it in a number of different ways, some crystalline and some in the form of small sheets, called 'glazed ice'. The motorist experiences icing on a freezing foggy morning, when the impact of the moisture-laden air on his windscreen causes a film of ice to form and stick to it and block his vision.

But below −10° C., icing seldom occurs. Thus the sailplane only experiences a build-up of ice for a fairly short period, as it climbs through the layer of air inside the cloud which is between the limiting temperatures, and during this time sufficient ice does not build up on the wings to be dangerous. It does not, like the aeroplane, fly for long periods at a steady altitude, and so the main problem is the icing-up of the pitot head.

The first solution to this problem was a small electric muff on the pitot tube, which is heated, when switched on, by dry batteries. The pilot waits until he has climbed above the icing layer, and then switches on for a minute or so, until the ice on the tube melts and blows off. After this he switches off, for the tiny batteries used will not provide heat for more than a few minutes, and ice will not form again unless he once more reaches the icing layer in cloud.

The second solution is to suppress the pitot head altogether, and drive the A.S.I. from a hole in the surface of the fuselage nose which is too large to be completely blocked by ice. The correct location of this orifice to ensure accurate readings at all speeds is, however, a rather tricky matter.

The oxygen problem is one of additional weight and expense, since the oxygen equipment used on fighter aircraft, although unnecessarily large and heavy, will do the job. The main problem was originally the psychological one of persuading the pilot that it was necessary.

Many aeroplane pilots used to say: 'Oh, I have been up to 20,000 feet without oxygen, and I was perfectly all right.' This attitude was overcome at the expense of many lives and much patience during the war.

Oxygen lack produces the same symptoms as excess of alcohol – a feeling of gay well-being allied to a progressive deterioration of the higher reasoning powers, culminating in a sudden black-out; and the same aftermath, in serious cases, of a headache and complete loss of memory of what happened.

In an aeroplane at 20,000 feet the higher reasoning powers may not always be required. In a sailplane in cumulonimbus, flying blind on a simple turn-and-bank indicator, they are, since the interpretation of the instrument is not natural but highly inferential. My own guess is that somewhere between 15,000 and 17,000 feet is the top limit for the normally respirated husband and father.

18

SUCCESS STORY

The following flight is the last high-performance sailplane flight which I have, at the date of writing, carried out, and it is interesting to compare it with the flight described in Chapter 2, which was my first effort, eighteen years before.

The first comparison is of the almost horrifying revolution in cost and complexity which has taken place. Whereas the Professor might have cost £150 all in, the Sky, with its instruments, oxygen, blind-flying equipment and radio in aircraft and retrieving car costs nearly twelve times as much.

Don't misunderstand me. One can glide, and have endless fun, for very much less: but if you want to assault the stars, it is nowadays a relatively expensive ambition.

But with full modern equipment an averagely competent pilot can, in averagely good English conditions, achieve flights much in excess of the world records standing in 1934, and fly safely in the turbulence and icing conditions of storm clouds in which the Professor would not have lasted for ten minutes.

The first flight was a vague dash downwind to an unknown destination; the last one a race to a previously set goal 77 miles away, reached at an average speed, on a fairly windless day, in excess of 50 m.p.h. with a climb in a storm cloud on the way to nearly five miles above sea-level.

Is this progress? There will always be some who deny it, but for myself I think that no good can come of such an attitude. The conquest of any part of Nature leads to increasingly complex machines and techniques, and it is through the slow victory of man's mind over matter that virtue can be acquired.

July 11th 1952 was the last flying day of the 1952 World Championships, held that year at Madrid. The four pilots of the British team were each flying the latest product of Slingsby, the 18-metre-span Sky, equipped with radio-telephonic communication between the aircraft and retrieving cars.

There were 56 starters, of whom 39 were in the single-seater, and the remainder in the two-seater class, and 19 competing nations.

The task was a race to Torresaviñan, a repetition of the 77-mile course flown a week before, and the weather forecast was good. There was a forecast of thunderstorms forming over the Sierras, but the Sierra de Guadarrama runs S.W.–N.E. to the north of Madrid, and as the forecast wind was west to all heights, and our course was around 060°, it did not seem likely that we should meet any cumulonimbus on our short flight. In the event, the upper wind produced a northerly drift which brought a very large storm over our course, and the height available in this storm (at least 30,000 feet and probably more) would certainly have made very long flights practicable. But it was quite impossible to have foreseen this up to the time of take-off.

Following our invariable routine, the trailers set off to traverse Madrid and await our first airborne messages at Barajas, the civil airport on the eastern side of the town. By 1.50, the time I took off, the ground temperature on the brown and dusty airfield at Cuatro Vientos was over

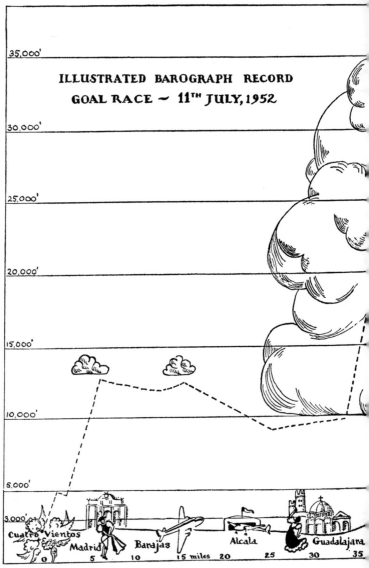

ILLUSTRATED BAROGRAPH RECORD
GOAL RACE ~ 11ᵀᴴ JULY, 1952

35,000'

30,000'

25,000'

20,000'

15,000'

10,000'

5,000'

3,000'

Cuatro Vientos Madrid Barajas Alcala Guadalajara

0   5   10   15 miles   20   25   30   35

28   *Cuatro Vientos to Torresaviñan*

206

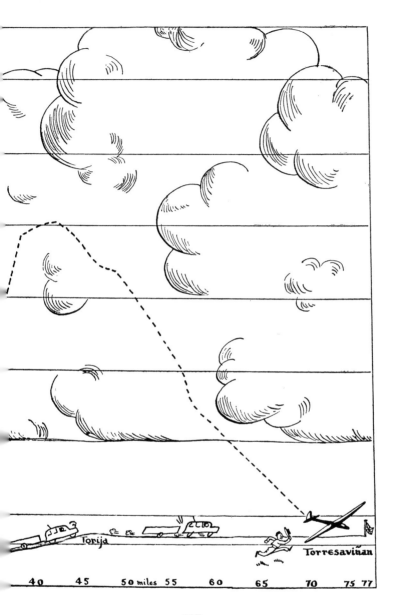

Torija

Torresaviñan

40   45   50 miles 55   60   65   70   75 77

100° F., and the first dots of high cumulus were beginning to show on the course, whilst cumulus developing to towering cumulo-nimbus had already been in evidence to the north along the line of the Sierras for some time. An unexpected sheet of high cloud started to drift south towards our course as I took off, which eventually grew to the aerial atomic explosion which ensued.

I was waved off, after an aero-tow to 1,500 feet, in a raging downcurrent, but flew straight ahead for the plantation of dark pine-trees which had proved to be a good source of upcurrents, and at 1,300 feet struck the usual 10 ft./sec. lift which took me up in a dancing cloud of sailplanes to 9,000 feet above sea-level.

I told 'Justin' (the call-sign of my retrieving team) that I was on my way. I crossed Madrid at a good height, and reached Barajas, 14 miles away, to find that the east-west sheet of high cloud drifting south from the Sierras was encroaching on the track, and tending to force me south of the course in order to keep within the sun and cumulus area. Thinking that this advance sheet of the storm cloud was unlikely to have lift under it, I kept south of it for a while, but by the time I reached a point south of Alcala de Henares, the east-west line of cloud cut right across my 60-degree course, and ahead over Guadalajara it looked as if it had developed into a definitely active state.

I therefore altered course to 030°, to get under the advanced edge, and immediately struck steady lift. I flew along under this edge for some miles, the lift gradually increasing from 9 to 15 feet a second, and over Guadalajara itself the leading edge of the cloud belled up into the customary dome-shaped undersurface which denotes big lift. I saw two Kranich sailplanes circling up into this dome, and under it the climb indicator hit the roof. Cloud-base within the dome was higher by at least 1,000 feet than elsewhere, and was reached at 10,500 feet. The two Kranichs had disappeared.

What to do? The task was a goal-race; I was half-way to the goal with about 35 miles to go. If I went into what was clearly 'big stuff' I might lose myself and miss my goal on coming out of the cloud. On the other hand, if I kept below it the course ahead lay diagonally under the cloud, and as I got farther back from the front (and lifting) edge, equally powerful compensating downcurrents might be met. I wanted my Height Diamond award – but this should weigh little beside the prospect of winning the World Championships.

Finally, I believe, instinct more than reason decided me – the instinct that, when Fortune is on your side, you should accept everything she offers; and the instinct, almost physically overpowering, which prevents a sailplane pilot from straightening up and flying out of lift over the top of the climb indicator. We circled on into the cloud.

I needed just over 20,000 feet on the altimeter for my Diamond height. Circling in dead-smooth lift over the top of the clock, we reached this height in no time at all, and I forced myself to straighten up on the course for Torresaviñan, expecting quickly to fly out of the area of rising air. We went on climbing.

It now became clear that I really was in something very big, and the unpleasant possibility came much nearer that I might go on higher and higher, and blinder and blinder, for miles and miles. Indeed, if the course that day had been the reciprocal, and I had been flying towards instead of away from Madrid, a straight course might well have kept me climbing to 35,000 or 40,000 feet for 50 miles or more; for the other end of the same storm passed over Cuatro Vientos, its leading edge, like a giant vacuum-cleaner, picking up so much dust that visibility for some time was down to three yards.

I turned south to try to fly out in front of the storm again, but went on climbing, still blind. I turned north for a bit, but realised that if I zigzagged about too much I should greatly increase the risk of emerging lost, and so returned to my 060° course, climbing all the time.

I wanted a good deal of information from 'Justin', but for the first time during the whole championships the ether seemed too full; not of storm noises – the Pye sets seemed utterly unaffected by static – but of all the rest of our teams speaking at once.

Pride of place in the concert was being taken by Jock Forbes. He had gone into the cloud without a barograph, and without oxygen, not realising what he was taking on, and was now over 18,000 feet. Too little oxygen produces the same symptoms as too much alcohol. Jock must be very talkative in his cups.

Behind this general curtain of sound, Lorne Welch was apparently in some trouble getting up into the high ground south-east of Guadalajara and was trying to instruct his ground-crew on how to keep close to him; whilst Stephenson, after making excellent time to within easy gliding distance of the goal, had run into the large area of violent down-current behind the storm, and was faced with the bitter disappointment of landing short. He was anxiously asking his ground-crew for the surface wind direction to enable him to pick a suitable landing-field, and they were having a hard time to answer at a time when the wind was waltzing round to all points of the compass like a merry-go-round, probably fanned on by Jock, who was now spinning out of the cloud in a chatty spiral.

I badly wanted to tell my ground-crew that I was now still climbing on a straight course, at over 20,000 feet, and so must guard against a serious risk of getting lost. Was there complete cloud-cover, and if so, what was the estimated height of cloud-base? This would give me some idea of how much height I would have to lose before seeing the ground again.

On the other hand I was, of course, on oxygen, and had to remove my mask to talk. I was not quite sure how long it would be at these heights, with my mask off, before I began to lose the keener edges of my mental powers, which are the first to go, and which were at the time badly needed. Long, thin, pale-blue sparks of static electricity were beginning to zip and prick from the quick-release cable to my left knee, and my main air-speed indicator had iced up. There did not seem to be much ice on the wings, but the entire inside of the perspex cockpit cover was covered with white rime, in which I scratched small holes when I wanted to look out. Although the cockpit is, in fact, only a narrowly fitting shell of thin plywood, it was warm enough inside in my tropical suit and light overalls.

I made one attempt to talk, but got a reply asking me to repeat my message in five minutes. This, I knew, meant that 'Justin' was rocketing up the last part of the gorge from Guadalajara to Torija, in which radio reception was poor.

The altimeter wound itself up to 24,000 feet and possibly beyond, but I had lost interest in it. I had now got my Diamond height, and the British Absolute Altitude and Gain of Height records (or so I thought, not realising that barographs could be so unco-operative),* and I knew in my bones that Fortune was not going to let me down.

And then we struck 'sink'. Never before have I been so cheered at finding myself coming down. Simultaneously, 'Justin' came through, and gave me the information I wanted: cloud cover complete, estimated height of cloud-base 10,000 feet. Minutes later, and the ground became dimly visible through a ragged hole beneath.

I dived down through this and anxiously peered around. I felt sure I had drifted south of the course, and flew north to contact the main road. In a few minutes I was able to radio that I had located myself. I had 14 miles to go with over 10,000 feet to lose in it. Diving as fast as I dared, I found, when my air-speed indicator started registering again, that I was approaching the goal at 120 m.p.h.

This is not exactly a classic way to finish a race, indicating as it does that time has been wasted in gaining unnecessary height and then in diving it off. But it sufficed. I shot over the finishing-line in 1 hour, 28½ minutes, to find myself World Champion.

Few people are fortunate enough to watch the story of Cinderella through to its conclusion, in real life. From 1932, when anyone taking up gliding was regarded as eccentric or suicidal or worse, British gliding has graduated, almost entirely on its own spirit and enthusiasm and hard work, to the position in 1953 when it is accepted by the public and, still more remarkable, by its more hard-bitten brethren in Service and civil flying, as a branch of aviation with a special value of its own.

* My first barograph failed, and my second went off the top of the chart after recording 22,430 feet – sufficient to gain the British Absolute Altitude record but not the Gain of Height record.

The gulf we have spanned has been enormous. In 1935 a highly influential and popular aviation paper published two leading articles on the subject of 'The uselessness of Gliding', ending with: 'Let us cut all this cant about gliding being of use to the nation. . . . And let us recognise gliding as a useless game which is therefore fit for gentlemen to play. . . . Then we shall know where we are.'

Almost exactly seventeen years later, the Minister of Transport and Civil Aviation, Mr Lennox-Boyd, held a reception at his house to welcome back the British team which had returned victorious from the 1952 World Championships, at which guests included four previous Civil Aviation ministers and many distinguished heads of Service and civil ministries. During the evening he read out a message from the Prime Minister:

'Pray congratulate on my behalf the British team who did so well in the International Gliding Championships, especially Mr Philip Wills who is now World Champion, and also the Slingsby Sailplane Company on the success of their gliders. Winston S. Churchill.'

We had come a long way, I thought, and now we had to make sure that what we had reached was not a peak but a plateau. There was still everything to do, but now we had the Powers That Be on our side, and all the people I liked and respected seemed with us, ready and eager to go on and ensure that it would be so.

And if the air of that Italian valley, deep and far-off and treacherously fair, was also in the room, that was for me only, that was a personal matter, like any sailplane pilot's sky.

EPILOGUE

This telegram from our Patron, the Duke of Edinburgh, was
received by me twenty-four years after the events described in the
last chapter. What are the developments in man, machine and
instrumentation which distinguish between a World Champion
in 1952 and one in 1976?

I think there has been an overall rise in the technique of
flying. Whereas in 1952 there was a small number of pilots head
and shoulders above the rest, now there are hundreds or even
thousands of pilots very nearly at the top of the tree. So all
honour to our new Champion, George Lee, for nowadays it is
much more difficult to be that little bit better than all the rest.

Something I find a little sad was also inevitable: the skill has
become more a technique and less an art. As knowledge expands,
the field remaining for inspiration contracts.

Competitions now consist almost entirely of closed-circuit
races, further restricting the choices available to the pilot. He takes
off from a grid, at a time dictated by the organisers. He cannot
cross the start-line until all are airborne. If he lands out, he cannot rush back for a second launch. Cloud flying is nearly always
prohibited. Thus some of the most interesting and demanding
skills of the 'complete pilot' are becoming redundant, and every
ounce of expertise has to go into speed-flying.

This, of course, has also affected the design of the aircraft, which today have speed performances beyond our wildest dreams in 1952. Also prices! My 1952 Sky cost, if I remember aright, the then horrifying sum of £1,100. With instruments added, the total may have reached £1,500. But a fully equipped 22m 1976 open class championship glider with instruments might easily set you back £20,000.

It will also be made of resin-bonded fibreglass, a material undreamed-of in our plywood days. Since it is possible with this material to produce very precise shapes quite unaffected by heat or cold, new families of wing-sections designed by Wortmann and Eppler have come into use. These have yielded a leap in performance in the order of that achieved in powered aircraft by the change from piston to jet engines. Once maximum gliding angles of 1 in 30 were an achievement: now angles of 1 in 50 are in sight. At higher speeds the improvement has been even more dramatic.

One slight snag is that these new wings are so susceptible to minor irregularities that performance is quite seriously reduced when the wing is wetted by rain, or if during take-off large numbers of insects get squashed on the leading edges.

Instruments, of course, have gone through the electronic roof since 1952. My simple perspex Slater-Cobb rate-of-climb indicator, with a little red ball in one tapered tube and a green ball in another, has now become an electronic brain capable of squeaking in an ascending pitch as I go up, telling me how fast to fly between thermals, and at the flick of a switch registering either total energy or air-mass movements. One gets the feeling that before very long it will take over the whole job, ringing an alarm bell to wake one up and pour out a cup of tea before landing. But in fact it isn't like that at all.

Speed flying has brought with it the unexpected need for

weight, provided by water-ballast to be jettisoned in poor conditions. The PIK 20B, which dominated the Standard Class in 1976, is a 15-metre ship with an empty weight of 540 lbs; it can carry no less than 300 lbs of water – equal to two extra human occupants!

The people who have lost out are the crews. Gone are the days when they drove all day to unknown destinations, found their pilot on inadequate information and a hunch, carried his aircraft out of impossible places and brought him dozing home through the night of a strange country. Often they can do no more than rig the aircraft, check their pilot over the start-line, then settle down for the first message of his final glide back to the finish.

But when all is said and done we still have the sport of all time. I started the first chapter in 1953 by trying to describe the fascination of gliding. Now nearly 70 years old, I have a little to add.

Gliding is the very reverse of what the ordinary man thinks. How often have people said to me 'It must be simply wonderful up there, in the silence and peace'. I'm pretty certain George Lee never even noticed the silence, and never experienced anything approaching peace, during any of his flights from Rayskalla. I know I didn't from Cuatro Vientos.

The total experience of belonging to the gliding community covers many factors and is enormously rewarding. There are many moments of beauty, of wonder and even of awe. But the real fascination of a successful flight in high competition is this. You have placed yourself in a situation of considerable stress, in a medium – the air – strange to your instinctive imperatives. You have given yourself exceedingly complex technical challenges. You are faced with a constant demand for a large number of rapid decisions, each to be made on the slenderest evidence. And, when you are in form, it all comes off – every decision turns out to be the right one. There *is* lift over that wood, in the lee of that small town or that sunward mountain side. The route that safely took you out to your turning-point is now closed to you on your return, because the sea breeze has penetrated ten miles further inland up the river estuary in the interval. But you notice the change of cloud-pattern and alter course accordingly. That cloud *is* lifting, the other is decaying. Elementary, my dear Watson. You find you have won. It all seems to have been so easy, you can't understand why the others found it so hard.

I suppose God feels like that, all the time. It only happens to a man once or twice in a lifetime.

BIBLIOGRAPHY

Gliding, considering the comparatively small number of people who partake in it, has evoked a surprisingly large literature. Here a few of the key books are listed. For a fuller list, write to the British Gliding Association, or subscribe to the US magazine *Soaring*, in which a large number of titles are advertised.

Free as a Bird. P. Wills
A personal account of 40 years of gliding as the author has known it, including stories of the battle against bureaucracy which must be carried on if we are to retain our freedom to fly

Gliding.   D. Piggott
Covers all aspects of gliding from the very first flight to advanced cross-country techniques

Pilots Weather. Ann Welch

Theory of Flight for Glider Pilots. R. C. Stafford Allen

Theory of Modern Cross Country Gliding. F. Weinholtz

Winning on the Wind. George Moffat
The ex-World Champion tells how to win competitions – ruthlessly

Sailplane and Gliding. The official publication of the BGA. Published alternate months, beginning December/January.

Soaring.
The American monthly journal, published by the Soaring Society of America, PO Box 66071, Los Angeles, Calif, 90066

Australia Gliding.
Monthly.   Box 1650 M, GPO, Adelaide, South Australia

Gliding Kiwi.
Bi-monthly.   PO Box 487, Taranga, New Zealand

THE BRITISH GLIDING ASSOCIATION

The BGA has achieved a high international status and such official regard that it has been allowed to control its own affairs to a greater degree than any other similar organisation.

It is the central association controlling gliding in Great Britain and all information regarding the location of gliding clubs in Britain and overseas can be obtained from the following address:

British Gliding Association,
Third Floor,
Kimberley House,
Vaughan Way,
Leicester.
Telephone number: Leicester 51051

BRITISH NATIONAL AND INTERNATIONAL
GLIDING RECORDS

To the list published in 1953, which gave the records standing in 1952, I have added the 1976 record under each heading. (The new kinds of records established since those days, when we never dreamed of 750km triangular speed-flights and suchlike, are not included.) Duration records were abolished shortly after 1952, when a French pilot was killed because he fell asleep after more than two days and nights in the air.

This list shows in a most interesting way where we have advanced, and where not. Duration, of course, becomes a nonsense. In Honolulu there is a mountain ridge up which the wind blows for 365 days a year. Gliding has nothing to do with the problems of feeding, exercising, sleeping and excretion which flights of such duration incur.

Height records are limited not by aircraft performance but by the oxygen-absorbing capacity of the blood. Until someone builds a pressure-cabin sailplane we can't go much higher. Where advance has exceeded all expectation has been in speed—and hence distance, which is a function of speed.

To retain the flavour of the book I have kept to the good old British units of measurement, not the metric.

SINGLE-SEATER DISTANCE

DATE	PILOT	SAILPLANE	MILES	ROUTE
4.9.32	Buxton	Falcon 1	13	Askam-in-Furness – Coniston
22.8.33	Collins	Professor	19	Dunstable – South Mimms
18.3.34	Wills	Professor	36	Dunstable – Latchingdon
5.8.34	Collins	Rhönadler	95	Dunstable – Holkham Bay

GLIDING RECORDS

DATE	PILOT	SAILPLANE	MILES	ROUTE
5.7.36	Wills	Hjordis	104	Dunstable – Pakefield
17.4.38	Nicholson	Rhönsperber	120	Huish – Bigbury-on-Sea
18.4.38	Fox	Rhönadler	145	Huish – Fowey
30.4.38	Wills	Minimoa	209	Heston – St Austell
13.7.47	Wingfield	Olympia	216	WichitaFalls – Buffalo Lake
1.5.49	Wills	Weihe	233	Hatfield – Gerrans
2.5.51	Bedford	Olympia	257	Farnborough – Newcastle
1.6.62	Lane	Skylark 3F	460	Geilenkirchen – Hiersac

World Records

5.8.51	Johnson (USA)		545	Odessa – Salina, Kansas
25.4.72	Grosse (WG)		908	Lubeck – Biarritz

SINGLE-SEATER GOAL FLIGHT

27.7.46	Wills	Weihe	113	White Waltham – Lasham
17.6.47	Wills	Weihe	140	Yeovilton – Ratcliffe
19.5.48	Forbes	Weihe	192	Fassberg – Cologne
19.5.48	Archbold	Weihe	192	Fassberg – Cologne
2.5.51	Bedford	Olympia	157	Farnborough – Newcastle
10.5.59	Goodhart	Skylark 3	360	Lasham – Portmoak

World Records

6.6.52	Efimenko (USSR)		395	Grabtsevo – Melovoe
16.4.74	Grosse (WG)		765	Lubeck – Marmande Virazeil

MULTI-SEATER DISTANCE

18.3.34	Collins & Exner	Kassel	46	Dunstable – Little Waltham
6.7.46	Sproule & Suthers	Kranich	103	Peplow – Owswick
17.6.47	Nicholson & Blake	Kranich	118	Yeovilton – Bramcote
28.5.49	Hirst & Simpson	Kranich	139	Gutersloh – Hamburg
1.8.76	Carlton & Spreckley	Calif.	394	Fairford – Luxembourg

World Records

17.7.38	Ilchenko (USSR) & Savtzov		385	Moscow – Ismailova – Ouchina
21.7.75	Renner (AUSTRALIA) & Geissler		603	Bendigo – Langley

MULTI-SEATER GOAL FLIGHT

DATE	PILOT	SAILPLANE	MILES	ROUTE
17.6.47	Nicholson & Blake	Kranich	118	Yeovilton – Bramcote
14.8.70	Fielden & Fielden	Bergfalke 3	262	Exeter – North Denes

World Records

19.7.51	Pawlikiewicz (POLAND)		318	Lesnica – Warcz
3.6.67	Gorokhova (USSR) & Koslova		539	In USSR

SINGLE-SEATER GOAL & RETURN

7.4.39	Murray	Rhönbussard	68	Ratcliffe – Castle Bromwich/rtn
16.7.47	Wingfield	Olympia	147	Wichita Falls – Quanah/rtn
3.6.51	Wills	Weihe	163	Redhill – Little Rissington/rtn
22.7.76	Garton	Kestrel 19	497	Lasham – Durham Cathedral/rtn

World Records

22.8.52	Coverdale (USA)		260	Grand Prairie – Brownwood/rtn
19.5.76	Striedeck (USA)		1016	Lockhaven – Oakridge/rtn

MULTI-SEATER GOAL & RETURN

12.8.49	Pringle & Grantham	Kranich	77	Cambridge – Dunstable/rtn
4.1.69	Warminger & Tucker	SGS 2-32	225	In South Africa

World Records

12.6.40	Kartachev (USSR) & Petrochenkova		309	Toula – Ouklevo/rtn
26.7.75	Minghelli (USA) & Gravance		467	In USA

SINGLE-SEATER GAIN OF HEIGHT

DATE	PILOT	SAILPLANE	FEET	STARTING-POINT
19.8.33	Collins	Professor	1,750	Dunstable
18.3.34	Wills	Professor	3,800	Dunstable

GLIDING RECORDS

DATE	PILOT	SAILPLANE	FEET	STARTING-POINT
5.8.34	Wills	Scud II	4,514	Sutton Bank
4.9.34	Buxton	Scud II	8,323	Sutton Bank
3.6.38	Wills	Minimoa	10,180	Dunstable
22.6.39	McLean	Grunau Baby	10,350	Hartside
1.7.39	Wills	Minimoa	14,170	Dunstable
23.6.46	Wills	Weihe	15,247	Long Mynd
24.8.50	Bedford	Olympia	19,120	Odiham
9.5.72	Field	Skylark 4	41,656	Booker

World Records

| 30.12.52 | Ivans (USA) | | 30,100 | Bishop, California |
| 25.2.61 | Bikle (USA) | | 42,303 | Bishop, California |

MULTI-SEATER GAIN OF HEIGHT

4.7.46	Furlong & Johnson	Kranich	3,601	Peplow, Salop
2.6.47	Williams & Kahn	Kranich	8,399	Oerlinghausen
24.7.49	Grantham & Bell	Kranich	10,080	Cambridge
16.8.52	Bedford & Austin	Kranich	12,750	Farnborough
3.2.70	Hood & Slater	KA 7	19,800	Issoire

World Records

| 29.3.52 | Edgar & Klieforth | (USA) | 34,426 | Bishop, California |
| 5.11.66 | Jozefczak & Tarczon | (Poland) | 38,500 | Tatry Mts. (Poland) |

SINGLE-SEATER ABSOLUTE ATTITUDE

24.7.50	Bedford	Olympia	21,340	Odiham
11.7.52	Wills	Sky	22,430	Madrid
9.5.72	Field	Skylark 4	42,900	Booker

World Records

| 30.12.50 | Ivans (USA) | | 42,220 | Bishop, California |
| 25.2.61 | Bikle (USA) | | 46.266 | Bishop, California |

MULTI-SEATER ABSOLUTE ALTITUDE

DATE	PILOT	SAILPLANE	FEET	STARTING-POINT
No British record in 1952				
5.1.67	Anne Burns & Janie Oesch	SGS 2-32	31,200	Bishop, California
World Records				
29.3.52	Edgar & Klieforth	(USA)	44,255	Bishop, California

SINGLE-SEATER SPEED OVER 100-KM TRIANGLE

DATE	PILOT	SAILPLANE	M.P.H.	COURSE
22.7.48	Wills	Gull IV	29.2	Muottas Murail – Weissflujoch – Piz Curver
19.10.75	Pearson	Nimbus 2	85.3	In Rhodesia
World Records				
28.8.52	Johnson (USA)		52	In USA
22.11.75	Goudriaan (S. Africa)		108.6	In South Africa

MULTI-SEATER SPEED OVER 1000-KM TRIANGLE

DATE	PILOT	SAILPLANE	M.P.H.	COURSE
No British record in 1925				
7.1.68	Pearson & Martin	Kranich III	52	Temple Clubhouse – De-Brug Station – Kaffir River Bridge
World Records				
13.8.52	Haase & Picchio	(WG)	50	In Germany
15.8.74	Holighaus & Plarne	(WG)	89	In Switzerland

SINGLE-SEATER DURATION

DATE	PILOT	SAILPLANE	HRS.	MINS.	SITE
18.8.38	Young	Falcon II	15	47	Long Mynd
World Record					
2–4.4.52	Atger (France)		56	15	Romanin-les-Alpilles
(Duration records abandoned)					

MULTI-SEATER DURATION

DATE	PILOT	SAILPLANE	HRS.	MINS.	SITE
9–10.7.38	Murray & Sproule	Falcon III	22	14	Dunstable
World Record					
4–6.2.52	Craaz & Branswyck	(France)	53	4	Romanin-les-Alpilles
(Duration records abandoned)					

INDEX